Can a Busy Christian Develop Her Spiritual Life?

········•◦•········

*Answers to
Questions Women
Ask About
Spirituality*

Answers to Questions Women Ask

Can I Control My Changing Emotions?
Can I Afford Time for Friendships?
Can a Busy Christian Develop Her Spiritual Life?

Can a Busy Christian Develop Her Spiritual Life?

Answers to Questions Women Ask About Spirituality

Kay Arthur

Jill Briscoe

Carole Mayhall

BETHANY HOUSE PUBLISHERS
Minneapolis, Minnesota 55438

Copyright © 1994
Christianity Today, Inc.
All Rights Reserved

Published by Bethany House Publishers
A Ministry of Bethany Fellowship, Inc.
11300 Hampshire Avenue South
Minneapolis, Minnesota 55438

Printed in the United States of America

Library of Congress Cataloging-in-Publication Data

Arthur, Kay, 1933–
    Can a busy Christian develop her spiritual life? / Kay Arthur, Jill Briscoe, Carole Mayhall.
        p.   cm.

    1. Women—Religious life.   2. Spiritual life—Christianity.
I. Briscoe, Jill.   II. Mayhall, Carole.   III. Title.
BV4527.A77   1994
248.8'43—dc20   94–27806
ISBN 1–55661–518–3   CIP

KAY ARTHUR and her husband, Jack, are founders of Precept Ministries. She reaches thousands weekly through the radio and television broadcast "How Can I Live" and is the author of eleven books and twenty-eight Bible studies, including *Lord, Where Are You When Bad Things Happen?*

JILL BRISCOE is the author of more than twenty books, including her most recent, *Heartbeat*, and *Marriage Matters*, which she wrote with her husband, Stuart. She is an internationally sought-after speaker and teacher.

CAROLE MAYHALL is a popular Christian communicator and author. She is the author of eight books, including *Help, Lord, My Whole Life Hurts*, and has served in the Navigators for more than thirty-five years with her husband, Jack.

Contents

Part Three
Understanding My Ministry

Epilogue

Introduction

Questions That Won't Go Away

WHEN IT COMES to the most vital and personal relationship of all—our walk with Christ—it's almost certain we'll have questions. Yet most of us feel uncomfortable asking, "Why do I sometimes wonder about my salvation?" or "Can I be angry with God?" or "Why does my spiritual life seem so difficult?"

We don't want others to question our commitment to Christ. And yet, we want the answers to these and other questions. In fact, we need the answers to develop a fuller relationship with God. Only by asking, reflecting, and applying answers do we make our faith our own. These simple but important steps allow us to cast off our misconceptions and bypass those stumbling blocks that make our spiritual life a burden rather than a joy.

In this book we've compiled seventeen of those difficult and often intensely private questions women ask. Then we consulted three wise and godly women—Kay Arthur, Jill Briscoe, and Carole Mayhall—for some answers.

Thankfully, they didn't provide yet another tidy "to-do" list for a fuller spiritual life. Instead, they looked back on their years of growing in the Lord and shared the lessons and insights they have learned. The result is open, honest, and, at times, challenging answers—ones that are certain to motivate you to dig into your Bible and renew your desire for a first-rate relationship with Christ.

The chapters in this book are based on personal interviews conducted in September 1991, and follow-up telephone interviews. Also featured in select chapters are excerpts from the pages of *Today's Christian Woman* magazine, as well as a section titled, "Make It Happen," which offers practical ways for you to quickly and easily implement the specific suggestions made in each chapter.

About the Contributors

Kay, Jill, and Carole are refreshingly straightforward in their counsel about the spiritual life. Each contributor has made the personal journey toward spiritual maturity—though they are quick to admit they have not yet reached the end. But they can attest to one fact—the rich rewards of an intimate relationship with the Lord are well worth the effort.

Kay Arthur and her husband, Jack, are founders of Precept Ministries, an organization whose goal is to establish God's people in His Word. Precept classes are taught throughout the United States and in seventy-four foreign countries. In addition to her duties as principal teacher at Precept, Kay reaches thousands weekly through the radio and television broadcast "How Can I Live?" Kay lives in Chattanooga, Tennessee, and is the author of several Bible studies, including *Lord, Where Are You When Bad Things Happen?* (Questar).

"Make your Bible your friend," advises Kay, in her instantly warm and charming manner. "I feel the Lord raised up Precept Ministries to teach people how to study God's Word for themselves so they can stand on their own two feet and then give insight to others. All my energies—all I write—is designed to get people into the Word of God and teach them how to know it for themselves." Her vitality and love for God's Word is contagious. While Kay is an amazing fountain of biblical insight and information, she remains an approachable, inviting, and inspiring woman of God.

Jill Briscoe is an internationally sought after speaker and teacher. She is the author of more than twenty books, including her most recent, *Heartbeat*, and *Marriage Matters* (both Shaw), which she co-wrote with her husband, Stuart. Jill was born in Liverpool, England. She and her husband ministered in England with the Capernwray Missionary Fellowship, a youth mission that spans the globe, from the time they were married until 1970. That year they moved to Waukesha, Wisconsin, where Stuart has served since that time as senior pastor of Elmbrook Church, a growing congregation that now numbers 6,000. When Jill is not traveling, she is deeply involved in the women's and media ministries at Elmbrook Church.

"I am self-taught," says Jill, referring to her biblical training. "You don't necessarily have to go to seminary or Bible school to gain knowledge of God. I have never had the opportunity to study for a concentrated period, but I have been able to take Bible courses along the way. Anyone can buy books and build into their busy life an ongoing and deep knowledge of God. Whether you're a man, woman, pastor, or layperson, we all ought to have a continuing biblical education with the goal of increasing our knowledge of God."

Jill's mince-no-words style is stimulating and challenging, but never intimidating. As you'll discover in her chapters, she's a thinker who makes others think.

———— ◌◌ ————

Carole Mayhall is a popular Christian communicator and author. She travels extensively, speaking at women's seminars and conferences on the topic of discipleship and marriage. She and her husband, Jack, live in Colorado Springs, Colorado, and together have served for more than thirty-five years with The Navigators, an international ministry organization that equips individuals in every nation to share the Gospel. Carole is the author of eight books, including *Help, Lord, My Whole Life*

Hurts (NavPress), and *Opposites Attack* (NavPress), a book about marriage, which she co-wrote with her husband.

Carole's practical nature clearly comes through in her chapters. She offers real-world advice for those struggling with their spiritual life, and she shares her wisdom with compassion and warmth.

"My prayer for myself and every woman would be that we approach the Word of God like children—standing on tiptoes, hardly able to contain our enthusiasm," says Carole. God has certainly used her prayer by making Carole's enthusiasm and devotion for the Lord an inspiration to others.

———— ✍ ————

As you read this book, it is our hope that you will find many "ah-ha" answers to your questions about the spiritual life. May you be encouraged and motivated to be the kind of woman God wants you to be.

Louise A. Ferrebee and
Marian V. Liautaud, Editors

PART ONE

UNDERSTANDING MY UNIQUENESS

ONE WOMAN THRIVES on emotionally intense and expressive worship where hands are raised upward and the murmur of "Yes, Lord" fills the air. Another finds comfort in the familiar words of a traditional liturgy and classical hymns. Yet another woman prefers a blend of both.

How we express ourselves spiritually and set our expectations for our spiritual life is as diverse as our personalities. Yet we sometimes wonder, "My spiritual life is so different from my friend's. Does that mean I'm less spiritual or that my approach isn't the best?"

Instead of dwelling on the differences, we should rejoice that God did not choose to fill His world with spiritual clones. Instead, He gave each one of us a wonderfully distinctive approach to worshiping, serving, and interpreting His Word. And it's that uniqueness that we should celebrate and cultivate.

In the following chapters, Kay, Carole, and Jill offer their stories on how they came to accept their unique spiritual style, as well as ways you can define and come to terms with your own. As Carole says, "God does not have spiritual grandchildren." We can't inherit a faith— it isn't something that can be passed on. The challenge is set—to make our faith distinctly our own.

1

Is There Only One Approach to the Spiritual Life?

—Kay Arthur

AS I WALK THROUGH the dining rooms during any of our Precept training workshops and survey the crowd, I can't help but smile. What diversity there is in the body of Jesus Christ.

I think, *Lord, how awesome you are! No one can put you in a box.* The Lord's children come in all shapes and forms, each with a unique personality. And I've witnessed the variety of ways others express their faith and relationship with the Lord.

If there were only one approach to the spiritual life, I might wonder as I look across the dining rooms, *Who among these hungry souls that have come to study the Word are the spiritual ones?* The exuberant, shiny-faced ones who intersperse their sentences with "Praise the Lord"? The ones who head for the books or lock themselves away in serious debates long after the meal is over? The ones who are eager to pray and sing His praises, yet find it hard to sit down and study? Surely it couldn't be those who take time for a game of tennis or visit malls? Or could it be?

Does countenance, interest, drive, or experience set any group aside as the "truly spiritual" ones? Do these actions or traits delineate spirituality?

There are some who would like to put God in a box, who define true spirituality according to certain dictates. It might be a code of behavior, a pattern of experiences, or a measure of exuberance. However, I have never found support for these mandates in Scripture or by biblical example. From what I see in the counsel of the Word of God, as well as what I've seen in the lives of dedicated Christians, is that true spirituality isn't achieved through keeping a rigid formula. It's not achieved by following a prescribed list of do's and don'ts. Nor is it achieved through squeezing God and His children into a mold.

WHAT'S THE BEST FIT?

Just as children within the same family are different, so children within the family of God are unique. There are common spiritual principles that can be applied in a hundred different ways. As you regularly read your Bible, use a colored pencil to underline principles like prayer or Bible study. Then ask yourself, "Where do I need to put this to work in my life?" Remember, the principles will be the same—it is the application that will differ.

—Jill

What does it mean to be spiritual? In the twenty-nine years I've walked with the Lord and come to know Him and His Word with some degree of intimacy, I believe the only approach to the spiritual life is through a *relationship*—a relationship with the Father, the Son, and the Holy Spirit.

This relationship is foundational. According to 1 Corinthians 3:10–11, it is the beginning of the only true source of the spiritual life. If your spiritual life begins

20

with a relationship and is based on that relationship, then it never can be maintained on the basis of a narrow system of do's and don'ts or a set series of experiences.

Three Keys to a Vital Relationship

Since Christianity is a relationship, not a religion, there are three basic tenets of the spiritual life that cannot be neglected if your relationship is going to be strong, vital, and vibrant. These tenets are time in the Word, communication through prayer, and involvement in those things of eternal concern to the Lord. To neglect all or any one of these three tenets is to neglect your spiritual life.

Without a doubt, Jesus is the best example of how we should approach our spiritual life. As you read through the Gospels and observe the Son's relationship to the Father, several things become evident. First, Jesus always carved out time to be alone with the Father. While the pressures of Jesus' ministry were great, that never stopped Him from making time to communicate with the Father in private—even if that meant finding time in the middle of the night.

Second, even from childhood Jesus was involved in what concerned the Father. When Jesus' parents were returning to Nazareth from a festival held in Jerusalem, they couldn't find Jesus. Where was He? In the temple at Jerusalem! And what did He say to His earthly parents when they questioned Him? He told them He had to be about His Father's business.

In His approximately thirty-three years on earth, Jesus constantly modeled for us the one true approach to the spiritual life. His governing passion was "for I always do the things that are pleasing to Him" (John 8:29, NASB). And how did he know what those things were? We could argue that He automatically knew them because He was God. But to say this is to miss the point. Although Jesus the man retained His deity, He walked as all men should walk—under the control of the Spirit.

Jesus knew what to do because He walked in the Spirit. He communicated with the Father and then did what was pleasing to Him. The words that the Father spoke, Jesus spoke. The works that the Father did, Jesus did. He was about His Father's business. As we read Jesus' words in John 8:28–29, "When you lift up the Son of Man, then you will know that I am *He*, and I do nothing on My own initiative, but I speak these things as the Father taught Me. And He who sent Me is with Me; He has not left Me alone, for I always do the things that are pleasing to Him" (NASB). Jesus allowed His relationship with the Father to govern His life—a relationship He nurtured through time and communion. This was His approach to the spiritual life, as it should be ours.

———— ✧ ————

When you and I carefully nurture our time with our Father, when we listen to His Word and talk with Him in prayer—seeking His counsel, wisdom, and will—then I believe we'll have a quiet confidence about our spirituality. We won't wonder if we're spiritual or not; we won't compare ourselves with others or their individual experiences. We'll just know we're right with God.

On the other hand, when we don't carve out time for serious study of His Word or we're too busy to pray, we'll find ourselves prone to equating spirituality with a list of do's and don'ts. If we don't allow God to be actively involved in our lives—even if we're going through the motions of church and other related activities—we'll begin to doubt our spirituality.

I can't emphasize enough that we are in a relationship with Jesus. Christianity is a relationship, and it takes time and commitment to cultivate and deepen that relationship. Don't neglect this relationship, my friend, for nothing is worth it.

Making Time, Taking Time

Just how much time do you need to spend in the Word of God and prayer? When should you do it? What time is best? Before you answer those questions, it's important to realize that true spirituality is a God-pleasing relationship between two individuals—it cannot be regimented or compartmentalized. Time alone—quiet, uninterrupted, unhurried—is necessary, but how much and when is something each one of us must work out on our own. The amount of time and time of day are not the issue, but rather, it is the quality of that time.

However, as I say this, let me share a word of warning. The trend these days is to promote spending five minutes a day in the Bible or in a devotional book, as if that were adequate. Granted, a few minutes is better than nothing. But since the spiritual life is a relationship, you need to realize you can't build a very solid foundation on five minutes a day—especially with God! How can you get to know God in only five minutes a day?

When you shortchange your time with the Lord, you make yourself vulnerable to erroneous teaching. You run the risk of misunderstanding the context in which things were written. You can't pick a verse here and another verse there, then put them together and say, "*This* is what will make me spiritual. *This* is what I need."

Such a piecemeal approach to studying the Bible is a lot like reaching into a promise box. Sure, you can pull out a promise and read it, but to whom was the promise made, and why? Are there any conditions to that promise? Likewise, you can read a devotion based on a single verse of Scripture and be ministered to, but a relationship is built on more than piecemeal information or conversations. Learn to move through the Bible book by book, so you have a context for what God is saying and you get the *whole* counsel of God.

———— ᥑᏯ ————

How much time you spend in God's Word and when you find that time will vary throughout your life depending on the constraints and demands you face. Thankfully, because spirituality is a matter of relationship rather than rules, you can set your own agenda.

HEADING IN THE RIGHT DIRECTION

From the air, downtown Washington, D.C., looks like a giant wheel with street-spokes leading to the Capitol. I wonder . . . from God's higher view, do our lives look something like that as we individually and uniquely approach the central core of the spiritual life?

—Carole

One of my heroes of faith, missionary Hudson Taylor, would rise about 4:00 A.M., spend time with the Lord, then go back to bed. I tried that. It didn't work. I have a dear friend who gets up at 5:00 A.M. I tried that, too, but my body clock wouldn't cooperate. I kept drifting off to sleep, which did nothing for my relationship with the Lord. Martin Luther used to spend four hours with the Lord first thing in the morning.

I spend hours in the Word, but it comes at varied times. As my leadership responsibilities have increased along with the span of our ministry, the battle for time has become greater. However, I must keep my time with the Lord as my foremost priority. I try to begin my day with Him—spending as much time as I can. Yet, if for some reason I don't get that precious time, I don't feel condemned or think God is displeased with me. He knows my heart, which is to spend time with Him.

Remember, the foundation of our spiritual life is a relationship that requires time and communion. If that relationship is important enough, you'll find time. You need to find a place to study God's Word and to communicate with Him in prayer and let Him speak to your heart—that's all that matters.

———— ✑ ————

When I've guarded the time that leads to intimacy with the Lord, when I'm deeply rooted in the Word and my prayer life is thriving, I am less prone to feel that my own spiritual journey is inferior or lacking just because someone else experiences God differently than I. Without a firm foundation of Scripture and prayer, I know that I, like others, can fall prey to every new trend that guarantees true spirituality. And then before long, instead of listening to God, I'm listening to whomever comes along claiming to have found what I may have been missing.

I am reminded of the words of Daniel, "but the people who know their God will display strength and take action" (v. 11:32b, NASB). When it comes to expressing ourselves spiritually, there is nothing new under the sun. But if we build on a solid foundation of reading our Bible and spending time in prayer, if we've taken the time to cultivate an intimate relationship with the Lord, then we can have confidence in how we live out our spiritual lives.

Make It Happen

1. Before you read another chapter of this book, take a few moments to reflect on your relationship with the Lord. Are the basics that Kay mentioned—studying and meditating on the Word of God and communion with Him through prayer—happening in your life? Start today with a promise that you'll begin these vital disciplines, and then reserve time for prayer and Bible study each day. Learn to view them as essentials in life, like a

good night's sleep or a healthy diet.

2. Write a brief autobiography of your spiritual life. What were the highs, the lows? When did you experience the most growth? The least growth? What is unique about your approach to the spiritual life? After completing your autobiography, praise God for the uniqueness of your relationship with Him.

3. If you wonder about how others express themselves spiritually, consider attending a different church service or function. How did it make you feel? Were there aspects in the worship experience that you would like to incorporate in your life? Rather than looking for comparisons, look for ideas and insights that would deepen your relationship with the Lord.

4. Consider reading biographies of noted Christian men and women for insights on how they approached their spiritual lives. Some names to consider are Henrietta Mears, Susannah Wesley, Hudson Taylor, Isobel Kuhn, or D. L. Moody.

How Would You Rate Your Spiritual Life?
Denise Turner

I haven't charted my spiritual life on a graph since I was a teenager, but I still remember the experience. Everyone in my group had almost identical graphs. The peaks were headed "summer camp." Everything else looked like one big valley.

I like to think I have come a long way since those early adolescent years. And yet, there are some days when I'm not really sure that I'm moving forward (or upward) spiritually. To assess my spiritual well-being, I need to consider the following questions.

- Am I comfortable enough in my relationship with Jesus Christ to talk with Him easily any time during the day— even when the baby is crying and the dog is barking and the soup is boiling over and I feel like He is a million miles away?
- Do I work at toning up my spiritual life regularly through prayer, Bible study, and outreach?
- Do I feel stronger in dealing with crisis situations than I did when I was a new Christian? Do I know in my heart that God is capable of keeping His promise to care for me?
- Am I an active member of my church, a church in which other Christians are willing to share with me, help build me up, and give me extra power to live my Christian life out in the world?
- Have I attended at least one meaningful Christian retreat or conference in the past three years?
- Am I assured of my salvation because my attitudes toward life are different than they were before I accepted

Christ? As one speaker put it, "I know I am a Christian whenever my heart is broken by the same things that break the heart of God."

- Do I start almost every morning asking the Lord, in one way or another, "What would you have me be and do today?"

—From *Today's Christian Woman* (March/April 1988)

2
How Do I Make My Faith Authentic?

—Carole Mayhall

I HAD TWO FEARS growing up. The first was my temper. As a child, I would often throw tantrums and become uncontrollably angry. This disturbed me and was frightening because I had no idea how to handle my rage.

My second fear was that when Jesus returned to gather up His own, which I had always been told He would do, I would be left behind. There were times I'd lie in bed at night, listening for my father's snoring. If I couldn't hear him, I'd creep into my parents' room and check to see if he was still there. The fear I would be left behind was that great.

One evening, when I was twelve, I came to the point where these two fears so overwhelmed me that I finally shared them with my mother. Once again, she explained to me the Good News of Jesus Christ. She reminded me that in Romans 3:23 it says we have all "sinned and fallen short of the glory of God." And in Romans 6:23, it goes on to say, "for the wages of sin is death, but the gift of God is eternal life in Christ Jesus our Lord." Jesus had paid the penalty for my sins by dying on the cross. He was the only one who could do that because He was sinless.

Later that night, I knelt down with my mother and asked Jesus into my life. From that moment on, the two things I feared most all those years were gone. I never had another tantrum and I knew Jesus would remember me in the end. While I still struggled with my temper, I never again experienced uncontrollable rage, and I have never doubted that when Jesus Christ comes back for His church, I will be included.

God doesn't have spiritual grandchildren. A relationship with Christ isn't something we can inherit or pass on. Each of us has to ask the Lord into our life on a personal level if we hope to have an authentic faith. Even though I was raised by a mother who would come out of her room with tears drying on her cheeks because she had been in prayer for me, and a father who showed Christlike patience as he cared for his senile mother-in-law, I had to take a step in faith alone. There's no doubt my parents' love and prayers were integral in bringing me to the point of accepting the Lord. But in the end, it was I who had to kneel before the Lord and ask Him into my life.

Claiming Jesus as our personal Savior is this first step of faith that sets us on a course toward an authentic relationship with Christ.

———— ✐ ————

If you were to chart my spiritual life from the point I became a Christian until now, it would look like a roller coaster. I went through several periods when I would get excited about my faith for a time, then my enthusiasm would wane. Even after becoming a pastor's wife and a homemaker, when everything looked right from the outside, I still felt something was missing from my spiritual life. Deep within my heart, I harbored two major concerns that I felt were holding me back from living an authentic Christian life.

First, surprisingly, was my marriage. When Jack and I got married, I knew it was God's job to make my husband good and my job to make him happy, but I thought God needed my help! At that time my philosophy was "faith without hints is dead." Unfortunately, my efforts didn't net a positive effect. Instead they brought about more frequent clashes between us.

If Jack did something I didn't like, I would clam up and become withdrawn. I used the silent treatment to punish Jack. Inevitably he would be forced to ask me what was wrong.

"Nothing," I'd lie, and then I would continue to ignore him. Jack knew I would grow more sullen if he didn't keep probing for the basis of my hostility. After he had exhausted all rational means of getting me to talk, and I felt I had punished him long enough, I would let him have it between the eyes. I would blast him verbally.

Consequently, he would either react with similar anger or withdraw completely. Many times it took until the wee hours of the morning for us to resolve our differences. Yet, even though we would forgive each other every time, deep down nothing changed.

At the same time my marriage was developing some serious problems, my spiritual life began to stagnate. Although I wouldn't have admitted it then, I was spiritually bored. Sure, I was grateful for my salvation and glad that I could talk to God about the big things in life, but the reality was there weren't many big things happening. My life consisted of dishes, dust, and diapers. And at that point, God wasn't the Lord of the everyday for me.

I knew there must be more to the Christian life than what I was experiencing, but I didn't know how to obtain it. After doing a lot of soul-searching, I began to realize that despite the fact I was raised in a Christian home, had attended Bible-teaching churches and went through seminary second-hand, much of the knowledge I had stuffed into my head had never dropped into my heart. Part of my faith was authentic, yet part of it consisted of going through the motions. I was living out a routine I had known since childhood.

HONESTY IS THE KEY

To make your faith authentic you must be honest. First, be honest when you pray. Second, be honest in your thought life. Third, be honest with your family and friends. Finally, be strict with yourself. Don't allow yourself to be "shoddy" in your Christian disciplines. Check your lifestyle. If you were watching yourself, would you consider yourself hypocritical? If so, be honest about it—then deal with it.

—Jill

While all this was happening in my life, Jack began meeting with a young man for personal discipleship. He spent hours watching this man and tapping into his practical knowledge. Frankly, I became jealous about the time he spent away from me, but then I began to notice changes in Jack and in the way he responded to me. During this time Jack and I had another familiar clash— this time right before he left for work one day. I stewed all day, and by the time he got home that night, I decided I wouldn't even greet him at the door with my usual hug and kiss. Instead I waited in the kitchen to make sure he knew I was still angry. As usual, we went through our routine where I withdrew, he questioned, I unleashed. But that's where Jack made a break in the cycle. Instead of becoming defensive, Jack looked at me with love and tenderness and said, "Well, Honey, maybe you're right. Let's pray about it together."

I felt like I was two inches tall. I couldn't pray, I couldn't get past my confusion. Finally after supper, I swallowed my pride, and I asked, "What enabled you to respond in a godly way to my anger?"

In that split-second after I had verbally assaulted

Jack, God spoke directly to his heart with the verse he had memorized from Hebrews 10:36, "For ye have need of patience, that, after ye have done the will of God, ye might receive the promise" (KJV). God changed Jack's heart from being defensive and vindictive to being filled with compassion.

Thanks to his friend's discipleship, Jack had begun hiding God's Word away in his heart. In the past, I had memorized Scripture too. In fact, at one time I had memorized 230 verses for a personal evangelism course. But the words never sank into my soul. Yet here was Jack memorizing the Word of God in a way that allowed him to apply it to any situation in his life.

That night I realized how far apart Jack and I were spiritually. I knew that if I didn't let God do something deep and significant in my life, soon Jack and I would be worlds apart.

Toward True Faith

In the weeks and months that followed, Jack shared his new knowledge with me and my spiritual life began to come alive. Like Jack, I took the first steps toward learning Scripture by heart. In fact, there's a big difference between memorizing something and knowing it by heart. And with Scripture, when you know it in your heart it has the power to change your life.

For instance, I also had a problem controlling my tongue when I would get angry. Yet I could never seem to break the habit of speaking out of anger until I learned Proverbs 18:2: "A fool gets no pleasure in understanding but only in expressing his opinion" (RSV). Those words were like a sword aimed directly at me. I cannot tell you how many times that verse has convicted me to hold my tongue when I would have liked to lash out at someone verbally.

Knowing God's Word by heart is a critical step toward maturing in the faith. Without it, you can be fairly certain your spiritual life will remain superficial.

TREASURED FRIENDS

As I worked on the *International Inductive Study Bible* (Harvest House), I had the opportunity to view the Bible as a whole. As I did so, my heart was touched as I read many familiar Bible passages. I felt as though I was pulling out old photographs and reminiscing. The passages were like treasured friends because I knew them, they were familiar and comforting, they went with experiences in my life. As I read a verse, I could remember when God illuminated it as I cried out to Him when I was hurting or our ministry was in need. Do you have treasured friends from God's Word?

—Kay

What made the greatest difference in opening up God's riches and making my faith authentic was examining my time alone with God. In my role as a minister's wife, I had certain expectations for myself and my spiritual life. One was that I should spend some time each morning reading the Bible and saying a prayer. I was faithful in meeting these goals, but half the time I didn't know what I was reading and my prayers were empty. I hadn't been *meeting God*. I had been meeting a habit.

Jack helped me break out of this cycle, too. He showed me that you have to come to God expectantly in the spirit of Psalm 119:18, "Open my eyes that I may see wonderful things in your law." Now when I study the Bible and pray, I come before the Lord expecting that He will have something to teach me. I spend more time listening for His voice instead of getting caught up in my own meaningless words.

And where I used to be concerned with the quantity of time I spent with the Lord, I now strive for quality—especially during chaotic periods in my life. Instead of reading a set number of chapters each day, I read a verse or a paragraph, but I read it meditatively, purposefully, with open ears so God can speak to me. Then I talk to God concerning the things He's spoken to me.

In fact, in those days I began to ask the Lord to show me my WT (Wondrous Thing) for the day. Sometimes He would give me a particular verse to help me during the day or an insight into Scripture. Whatever the Wondrous Thing happened to be, the important thing was that I anticipated His presence in my life. I expected big things of God.

Part of what makes a faith authentic, of knowing your walk with the Lord is "real," is knowing that God is speaking to you in a personal way on a continuous basis. And each day as I came across yet another Wondrous Thing, I knew God cared about me, and my faith was my own.

———— ∽ ————

It's easy, I have discovered, to fall back into a "habit" time with God. What helped me move beyond this erratic kind of relationship was to ask God for a hunger for His Word, a thirst for His righteousness. We have to remember that the enemy doesn't want us to walk with God. When an extra hour opens up in our day—a perfect hour to be with the Lord—we have a choice as to how to spend it. Unless we have a deep need to know God better and cultivate our relationship with Him, we could easily choose to spend our free time doing housework or making phone calls.

Unshakable Cornerstone

It's important to remember that our faith becomes authentic in the dailies of life, not through a big trial or grand challenge. In Colossians 3:17 Paul reminds us, "And whatever you do, whether in word or deed, do it all in the name of the Lord Jesus, giving thanks to God the Father through him."

That includes all things. After Jack left his associate pastor's position, we moved to California where he ran a center for U.S. servicemen. My days were filled with scrubbing floors, making beds, and preparing meals for a crew of servicemen.

It was there that I realized a good work is anything you do in the name of the Lord. I could scrub my floor for the Lord. I could prepare my meals for the Lord. I could take care of my child for the Lord. Everything I did, no matter how mundane, became a way to fulfill my calling as a child of God. Approaching my role in life like this gave me a whole different perspective.

---------- ✑ ----------

Ephesians 3:14–19 spells out the bottom line in making our faith authentic: "When I think of the wisdom and scope of his plan I fall down on my knees and pray to the Father of all the great family of God—some of them already in heaven and some down here on earth—that out of his glorious, unlimited resources he will give you the mighty inner strengthening of the Holy Spirit. And I pray that Christ will be more and more at home in your hearts, living within you as you trust in him. May your roots go down deep into the soil of God's marvelous love; and may you be able to feel and understand, as all God's children should, how long, how wide, how deep, and how high his love really is; and to experience this love for yourselves, though it is so great that you will never see the end of it or fully know or understand it. And so at last you will be filled up with God himself" (TLB).

According to the apostle Paul, our goal in life is to know God's love. The Living Bible translation of this verse uses the words *feel*, *understand*, and *experience* when it refers to this process. I have discovered one way to begin to truly know God's love is by learning His Word by *heart*. Then, combined with our personal acceptance of Christ, spending quality time with the Lord daily, and serving Him heartily in the dailies of life, we can be confident that our faith is indeed authentic.

Make It Happen

1. Start today looking for that WT (Wondrous Thing) in your times with God. Consider adding an extra page to your prayer notebook to keep a list of those Wondrous Things. How have they challenged or changed you spiritually?

2. Trace back your Christian heritage by talking with parents and other relatives about their Christian walk. What were some turning points in their lives? How did they come to their own personal relationship with the Lord? What are the parallels to your life, and what is different in your walk that makes it individual and unique?

3. As you learn Scripture by heart and come before the Lord with an eagerness to receive His Word, keep a record of how He is working in your life. What changes are taking place? Sometimes in the busyness of our days we can't see how active and involved God is in our life. Take the time to jot down a few lines that outline specifically how God is changing you to be more like Him. Use this list as a source of encouragement on those days when you feel down and discouraged.

3

How Can I Discover and Learn to Appreciate My Gifts and Talents?

—Jill Briscoe

I ONCE HEARD a woman say, "My gifts won't make me a Mother Teresa, so how can I see them as something special that can be used for God's Kingdom?"

Who of us hasn't felt less gifted than Mother Teresa. Yet the simple truth is this: If God had wanted us all to have Mother Teresa's gifts, He would have made us all just like her. Instead God chose to hand-make each one of us. And just as a potter works with his clay until the piece takes exactly the right shape for the purpose it is intended to serve, so God creates us.

What a beautiful image the Lord gives us to understand that He has crafted each of us *perfectly* for the role He has in mind for us. Psalm 139 describes how God formed us within our mother's womb. He knit us together in unique ways so each of us would be perfectly equipped to fulfill His purpose for us. This is an essential concept to grasp because, before we can begin to utilize our skills and abilities, we have to believe that God has blessed each of us abundantly with specific gifts to be used for His glory. Without this understanding, it is all too easy to fall into the trap of comparing our gifts to others, as the woman I mentioned earlier was doing. Though some people gain recognition for their talents or serve in more visible ways, no one gift carries greater value than another.

We are *different*—that's the key word. We possess different gifts and different talents, not better or best gifts and talents.

———— ∽ ————

The New Testament refers to hidden gifts in people, much like hidden members of the body. Take the heart, for instance. You can't see it, but in reality the heart is as important as the body parts we can see—like a hand or an eye.

And so it is with spiritual gifts. Many times it is the hidden gifts that are absolutely essential, though often they are the ones that go unsung. For instance, consider the support efforts in the church, like secretarial work, preparing meals, or decorating the altar for Sunday worship. Though these may seem like insignificant contributions to the church, they are, in fact, the efforts that make the whole body run smoothly. Without these gifts in action, the more visible parts of the body would suffer.

As one of the directors of our church's media ministries, I am responsible for many of the ideas and concepts we communicate. I do the speaking for our television program and write the scripts for our church dramas. I am probably the most visible part of the ministry, yet we have a video team of two dozen women who perform critical tasks—not to mention the dozens of members of the drama team. Without these people, this ministry could not function. I can share all the biblical insights I want on camera. But if the women behind the cameras aren't performing their jobs our ministry doesn't have a chance of fulfilling its purpose. The behind-the-scenes gifts are different, though no less important, than the visible gifts. We need each other. We need all the gifts working together if the body of Christ is to function as God intended.

Unwrapping the Package

The best way to begin to discover your gifts is to forget about them. Drop any preconceived notions you may have about your talents or interests. Next, look around your church or community for a need. Study the Sunday bulletin and see where help is needed. Check your local newspaper to learn about volunteer opportunities. Then ask yourself, "Could I do that?"

If your immediate reaction is, "No," consider this: "How do you know if you've never tried?" Too often we make excuses for not getting involved by saying, "Oh, I couldn't do that. It's not my gift." But the fact is, you can't hope to uncover a gift unless you're willing to explore new territory.

My husband, Stuart, is the best example of someone who discovered a natural talent by trying something new—something he really didn't want to do. When he was seventeen, a man came up to him while he was standing at the back of the church.

"It's time you were preaching," said the man.

"I can't preach," said Stuart.

"How do you know? Have you ever tried?"

"No."

"Then how do you know you can't? You will preach next week to the youth group. And your subject is the church at Ephesus," said the man as he walked away.

At that point, Stuart wasn't sure there was a church at Ephesus. But he did some research, prepared a talk, and gave it a try. At that time, many churches in his area were without pastors. The church leaders asked Stuart to take his sermon on the road and visit the neighboring communities. After completing his first preaching circuit, every church asked Stuart back and he had to get a new talk! He has never stopped preaching since.

––––––– ∽ –––––––

Stuart discovered a gift he didn't know he had because he was willing and obedient to offer help where it was needed. He could have easily declined to preach to that youth group, as most of us would who have never spoken to a group before. But Stuart didn't let his in-experience stand in the way of serving the Lord. That's something we all need to remember as we look for ways to use our talents. Gifts are seldom polished and refined when we first try them out. In fact, most of the gifts I have discovered for myself grew out of a willingness to help, regardless of how well I thought I could perform the job.

For example, I had no idea I could write drama scripts until I was helping out at a teenage mission in the back streets of Liverpool, England. The leader of the mission asked me to put together a nativity play. I wrote the script, discovered it worked—despite a lack of quality and content—and the following year I got the job of writing more scripts. With practice I became better and here I am today, still writing scripts.

FROM A LOVING FATHER'S HAND

Personally, I began to comprehend my gifts through trial and error, experience, counsel, evaluation, and finding out what God especially blessed and drew me to. But appreciating them was another matter!

To appreciate the gift(s) God has given me, I had to accept them as from a loving Father's hand, refuse to compare myself with others, and learn what my unique place was in the body of Christ. Believe me, it sounds easier than it was!

—Carole

Surprisingly, sometimes when we perform a task poorly, it helps point out others' strengths. For example, I don't have a talent for hostessing—of making my home a comfortable and inviting place for company. I'm sure, after the first few times I tried entertaining, some of my friends said, "She needs help." Sure enough, the next time I invited people over, one woman offered to serve the coffee. Another volunteered to prepare the food, and still another woman said she would make the table decorations.

I could have easily let my pride get in the way and continued to do a miserable job at entertaining or forgo inviting people into my home altogether. Instead, I was able to recognize and accept the fact that entertaining simply is not where my talents lie. While I may be able to open my home to strangers and visitors, I need others who have a stronger sense of hostessing to help me make entertaining a positive experience for everyone.

-------- ∽ --------

Sometimes our gifts never have a chance to reveal themselves because we fear failure. We fall victim to the mindset "If I can't do it well, I won't do it at all." Unfortunately, I think, American women, in particular, have a hard time viewing failure as a natural part of growth.

When my book *How to Fail Successfully* was released in the States, it did miserably. The publisher attributed the book's failure to its title. Yet the same book proved to be a bestseller among British readers *because* of the title!

I'm convinced that American women are so afraid of looking stupid that they won't even try something unless they are certain they will succeed. Interestingly, Europeans seem to hold the opposite attitude. They say, "Okay, I failed. How can I do it better next time?"

Failures help us learn how to do something right. As we discover our gifts, we must be open to failure. Look at a child learning to ride a bike. He will fall hundreds of times. Yet seldom does a child throw the bike aside and say, "I'm never trying that again!"

The Bible says whatever you do, do it heartily. It

doesn't tell us to do everything well. We've got to learn to say, "I'll start doing it badly for Jesus. I don't care if I make a mess of it. I'm just going to do it courageously." It's with this approach we can discover and polish our God-given gifts.

Joy of Discovery

God created us to enjoy the gifts we possess. In fact, one way you can determine whether you are exercising a God-given gift is by the level of enjoyment you derive from it. Not long ago a woman I know beautifully decorated a table, and I commented on how pretty and inviting it looked. She just shrugged her shoulders and said, "Oh, it's easy. I love doing this—it's my thing."

Clearly, this was her gift even though she simply viewed it as something fun to do. It's important to remember that God gives us innate desires and talents to help guide us to the areas where He wants us to serve. As you begin to fill needs in your church, be attuned to the tasks or activities that give you great pleasure.

Likewise, if you are engaged in functions and tasks that are a drudgery, chances are that is not where your gifts lie. Of course, you have to try a new endeavor long enough to know for sure whether you are suited to the job or not. But inevitably, as you try to uncover your strengths, you will come across areas that simply are not a good fit for you.

A Question of Obedience

We all carry preconceived notions about what we feel our strengths and weaknesses are. No matter what limitations we think we have, God still asks us to be obedient to His will and His Word. For instance, 1 Peter 4:9–10 instructs us to "offer hospitality to one another without grumbling. Each one should use whatever gift he has received to serve others, faithfully administering God's grace in its various forms."

VARIETY IS THE SPICE OF LIFE

God has a world to reach and He's not going to reach it through one individual. Rather, He is going to reach the world through a multitude of individuals with different personalities and gifts. In the Bible we see Peter and John who were called "sons of thunder." There was Nathanael "in whom there is no guile" (John 1:47, NASB). God used all these different apostles to reach the world and continues today to use a variety of people.

—Kay

Although hostessing is not my strong suit, I am still required by God to offer it. I remember a time when a missionary friend wrote asking me to invite her daughter, who attended college with my daughter, to our home for Easter. In all honesty, I didn't want company—I wanted that time just for our family. I wrestled over my decision, but in the end, I consented to my friend's request. Soon, what began as one extra guest turned into six extra visitors.

It wasn't until much later that I learned one of these students had helped my daughter through some very rough times spiritually. I can't tell you how thankful I was to be able to reciprocate some of the caring my daughter had received.

This incident was a real lesson to me. I secretly didn't want to be that hostess—it doesn't come naturally to me. But those young women had parents who were far away serving as missionaries. They needed someone to welcome them in like a mother. And although hostessing

45

may not be my gift, I am called to obey the Lord and do the job as best I can.

An Encouraging Word

Of the gifts I feel God has blessed me with, the one I am most thankful for, and which gives me the greatest joy to use, is the gift of encouraging and nurturing others—especially women. There is nothing that compares to the thrill of tapping a woman on the shoulder and saying, "Will you try this? I know you can do it. I'll come alongside and we'll do it together."

I've always been active in our church's counseling ministry. Some years ago, I noticed that whenever I was too busy to counsel those who were waiting in line to speak to me after I had taught a Bible study, the people would get up and go talk with a woman who was sitting nearby. I finally walked up to this woman and said, "I've noticed that people keep coming over to talk to you when I can't help them. You have counseling gifts."

"Oh, not me," she said, "I'm just waiting to take a friend home."

"But listening like you do is a gift," I assured her. "And it's a gift that is transferable to so many activities."

That conversation took place fifteen years ago. Since that time, this woman became the initiator and head trainer of the women's counseling ministry at our church. What I saw was a good listener—the raw material of a gift that could be put to use for the church.

Gifts often surface with a little prompting. I think that's why I get so much enjoyment out of being a nurturer—someone who will prompt others to cultivate their talents. I love to see people discover their gifts and begin to fulfill their potential.

One woman came to our church very broken. Fresh from a divorce, she had no idea where she'd fit in our large congregation. But she saw in the bulletin a need for kitchen help, and she thought, "I can wash dishes.

46

That's where I can enter this big body of people and start to heal."

At first she served in the kitchen without much notice. But then things began to happen; most notably, everyone was signing up for the kitchen committee—a first in our church's history.

When I asked the leader of our women's ministries why there had been such a surge of interest in this area, she told me about the woman who had begun as an unassuming dishwasher. Apparently, this woman had taken over the job of managing the kitchen committee, she worked well with people, listened to their troubles, and was exceedingly efficient and detail-oriented.

Once I heard this, we decided to give her some additional responsibilities. Before long, this woman had coordinated our women's day program that nearly 1,000 women attended. Then she organized a women's breakaway weekend at a local hotel, followed by a leadership conference. She even coordinated Joni Eareckson Tada's visit to the city of Milwaukee.

And she started in the kitchen. With the encouragement of others, her many gifts—organization, listening, punctuality, efficiency, and an eye for details—were transferred to larger areas of responsibility.

When the Gift Doesn't Fit the Niche

God gives us talents and gifts and holds us accountable for them. One day we'll stand in front of God and answer for the way we have used them. Therefore, if He has given me a talent, it is my responsibility to figure out a way to use it. If some people don't want me to use it in one place, then I have to ask myself, "How can I function? How can I use it?" It won't always be easy finding that niche.

Ideally, a woman will be able to exercise her gifts within the role she chooses to fulfill. A natural patience with children might flow into serving as a preschool teacher. However, there are some instances when women are not able to use their gifts within the context of the church community. If that happens to be your case, then search for creative alternatives within the fellowship of believers where your gifts can be utilized and developed. Or consider looking for a niche in a parachurch organization, such as a community outreach program where your gifts can be comfortably and acceptably exercised.

Even before I became a Christian, there was no doubt I had a natural talent for speaking. When I became a Christian I wanted to use this ability in a spiritual environment, but theologically that wasn't accepted by the ministry organization in which Stuart and I were involved. Because I believed God gave me a voice for a purpose, I decided to use my gift where I could. I began sharing the Gospel on street corners and got involved in open-air evangelism.

Eventually, after hearing me speak on the street, I was invited to use my talent for the ministry. My gift was affirmed by the mission and I was given a place to use it within the organization.

———— ✍ ————

There will always be a place where God's gifts can be used. It might not be where you'd like it to be, and some might not accept what you have to offer, but whatever the challenges you face in trying to find a niche to share and cultivate your gifts, the responsibility to do so is yours.

During World War II Winston Churchill said, "Give us the tools, and we'll finish the job." God has given us the tools—our gifts—to finish the job. And just as the Allies worked together in the war effort, so each of us is uniquely qualified to work together and to fight for the Lord in evangelizing the world. And in the end, when we stand before God, we will have to account for the way we used the gifts He gave us. It is up to us to discover those unique and special gifts and then put them to use for His glory.

Make It Happen

1. Point out a gift you see in a friend or a fellow church member. Be open and honest in your encouragement. Be persistent. Remember, you see others differently from how they see themselves.

2. Make a list of those things you most enjoy doing. Share your list with your spouse or a close friend. Do they have other ideas to add to the list? Do they question some of your entries? From this list, look for a common theme running through those things you enjoy. Is it organizing? Listening to others? Entertaining? Highlight the areas that seem to be your unique gifts.

3. Once you've identified your gifts, have a goal in mind with how you might use them. Don't spend too long planning, however. You will learn more by jumping in and getting your feet wet.

4
How Do I Keep My Faith Fresh?

—Carole Mayhall

THERE'S NO DOUBT THAT our faith can become predictable and routine. After all, our spiritual life is a relationship and, like any relationship, we can expect it to go through cycles—highs and lows. However, we can choose to rejuvenate it when the lows hit rather than panic or feel hypocritical. Because God so loves us and wants us to be in a close and growing relationship with Him, we don't have to settle for anything less than a fresh faith. Over the years, three factors have helped me keep my faith growing and alive—focus, outreach, and courage.

———— ∽ ————

Focusing on the things of God is integral to keeping our faith fresh. Yet I never realized its importance until a series of events occurred and the Lord revealed to me some key verses from His Word.

First I heard a story about a man who was *the* expert in spotting counterfeit money. When asked how he became so good he said, "I spent hours and hours each day studying the real thing." What a simple truth: If you want to know the real thing, study the real thing. Yet how many of us as Christians focus on peripheral aspects of our faith rather than studying the real thing: Christ himself through the Word of God. We need to focus on the perfect Christ rather than on man and our imperfect world. And by keeping our eyes on God, our faith will stand firm even when everything else fails us.

The second event that spoke to me occurred while I was getting my hair done at a Colorado Springs beauty salon. I overheard three women talking about what they would do if there were a nuclear attack. This is a real threat in our area because underneath Cheyenne Mountain, which overlooks our city, is the North American Air Defense command center. If there is a nuclear attack, Colorado Springs would likely be a primary target.

The first woman said, "There's no point in running. You can't get away. I'll just stay set." They agreed on that fact. Then the second woman said, "I hope I'm in bed with someone I love."

The third woman, who had obviously been dieting all her life, added, "I'm going to keep a giant hot fudge sundae in my freezer. When the sirens go off, I'm going to run to my refrigerator and eat everything in sight."

Of course, they all broke up laughing at this last woman's comment. But as I listened, I realized that behind their comments was an undercurrent of fear. They were afraid because of their focus—the threat of nuclear destruction.

———— ⟋⟍ ————

After this incident, I realized I had some questions that needed answers. One day I cried out, "Lord, I do not want my focus to be on my problems and my fears. I want to focus on what you want me to focus on. But I need to know what that is and how to do it."

God led me directly to Colossians 3, and it was as though the Lord had grabbed hold of me, shaken me, and said, "Take special note." I had memorized these verses years ago, but at that moment they *dropped into my soul*. I read in my Bible, "Since, then, you have been raised with Christ, set your hearts on things above, where Christ is seated at the right hand of God. Set your minds on things above, not on earthly things" (Colossians 3:1–2).

That was it. To keep my faith fresh, I need to "set my heart (my emotions) and my mind (my thoughts, my intellect) on things above." That means the total Carole is to be focused *up*, not *out*.

I said, "Oh, Lord, that's what I *want*. But how do I really do that?"

And God said, "Read on."

As I reflected on the following verses, I realized that if I wanted to keep my focus on Christ, a prerequisite was to unclutter my mind, get rid of the uglies in my life, and then clothe myself in what is good. Now, I admit, it's a long-term project to live by Colossians 3:8–10, "But now you must rid yourselves of all such things as these: anger, rage, malice, slander, and filthy language from your lips. Do not lie to each other, since you have taken off your old self with its practices and have put on the new self, which is being renewed in knowledge in the image of its Creator." I'm helpless to do that without the help of the Holy Spirit working within me. But *my will* is involved. I am to "rid myself" and "clothe myself."

I whispered again to the Father, "All right, Lord. I think I'm seeing what you mean. In order to focus on you, I need to continually work at getting rid of all those uglies in my life and to clothe myself with all the beautiful things you want to see there. But, Father, you still haven't shown me *how* to do that!"

Once again the Father said to my heart, "Carole, *read on.*"

And suddenly there it was—a verse I knew but didn't *know*. A verse that is the bottom line of the "Yes, but how?" question I asked. My focus needed to be on Jesus. The verse capitalized itself in my mind: "LET THE WORD OF CHRIST DWELL IN YOU RICHLY . . ." (v. 16).

I realized suddenly that often I dwell shallowly—not *richly*. And my ability to keep my focus on Jesus is directly related to His Word dwelling within me. When we dwell richly in His Word, we can experience daily those wonderful things—a verse just for us, an answer to prayer. And it's those daily occurrences that keep our focus constant and our faith ever new and exciting.

I just wrote, "keep our focus constant . . ." but in actuality, that isn't completely possible for us. Not long after reading Colossians 3, I said to a good friend, "More than anything, I want my focus to be on Christ, yet inevitably my focus strays. I stay focused for a time, but then some problem comes up and distracts me from Him again."

My friend offered this insight. "We're too human, aren't we—to *always* keep focused. But I think what we need to aim for, Carole, is shorter and shorter 'lapse time.'"

Exactly.

NO EASY FORMULA

The problem with formulas for the spiritual life is that they don't work—because everyone is different and unique. And because each person is different, what keeps me fresh may not work for another person. There is a danger in reading a book that kept one person fresh and assuming it will work for you as well. You have to know yourself and what works for you in order to keep your faith fresh.

—Jill

Our thought life has everything to do with focusing. A few years ago Jack and I were involved in a heart-breaking situation. A pastor friend had left his wife for his secretary and we tried to offer counsel. The situation occurred just before our annual two-week trip to the mountains—a time Jack and I greatly look forward to and reserve for study, prayer, and writing.

Yet as I walked the mountain roads that first morning, my heart felt heavy. *What was the matter with me? I wondered.* I was so looking forward to this wonderful getaway, yet I felt depressed. When I did a little digging, I realized I was still preoccupied with the situation between our friends. Then the Lord reminded me, "Whatever is true, whatever is noble, whatever is right, whatever is pure, whatever is lovely, whatever is admirable—if anything is excellent or praiseworthy—think about such things" (Philippians 4:8).

The Lord questioned my heart, "Carole, what you are thinking about—is it true?"

The Lord took me through the whole list—admirable, excellent, praiseworthy, and I realized that the thoughts I was brewing met only one of the eight qualifications on this list. Not good!

The Lord pointed out that even though the circumstances were heavy on my heart, I couldn't do anything about it. I had to leave it with Him. Every time the situation came back in my mind, I needed to pray about it and turn it over to the Lord. Otherwise, I wouldn't be able to keep my focus on those things above.

The only way to achieve a true sense of peace and joy is to free our minds of the world's preoccupations and concentrate on making our time with the Lord fruitful. Meditation is one of the biggest keys to dwelling richly.

———— ✐ ————

I suffer from insomnia. When my body says, "Goodnight," my mind says, "Hello, there." While it's frustrating to lay awake in bed, it does give me time to dwell on Scripture. And through the years I've found that to allow the Word of Christ to dwell deeply in you, you need to meditate on it.

Meditation to me is taking small segments of the Bible and reflecting on how they apply to your life. Most of us meditate casually—we think as we read, study, or listen. But as it says in Psalm 1, we should be meditating on God's Word day and night—and in more than just a casual sense.

Unfortunately, most of us don't know how to meditate on the Word. One technique that helped me learn to memorize and meditate on Scripture was to approach it systematically. Someone once told me that they used the vowels—AEIOU—to aid them in meditating. I put the idea to work and since that day it has made a tremendous difference in how I learn Scripture.

The system is simple. *A* is for *ask questions*. What is the verse saying? Who is saying it and why? *E* is for *emphasize certain words*. For instance, "*The* Lord is my shepherd." "The *Lord* is my shepherd." "The Lord *is* my shepherd." "The Lord is *my* shepherd." And finally, "The Lord is my *shepherd*." *I* is for *illustrations*. For instance, the verse above can be further ingrained in the memory by touching your thumb for "the," your index finger for "Lord," and so on. *O* is for *other verses* that relate to this verse. Review them in your mind and consider how they shed light on the verse you are meditating on. *U* is for *use* or application. How are you going to use this verse in your life?

When you are driving, doing laundry, whenever your mind is free, consciously and deliberately take a verse of Scripture that you have memorized and meditate on it.

Reaching Out

She floated down the stairs, sat on the bottom step, and breathed, "I'm in love." She didn't have to tell me! It oozed out of every pore! And for the next thirty minutes, I heard *all* about the man of her dreams. Rare is the newly engaged person who fails to extol—at length—the virtues of the chosen one. It is the natural thing to do.

When we really fall in love with Jesus, something of

the same thing happens. As Paul proclaims in Colossians 1:28, "So, *naturally*, we proclaim Christ! We warn everyone we meet, and we teach everyone we can, all that we know about him, so that, if possible, we may bring every man up to his full maturity in Christ Jesus" (Phillips).

If we are *really* focusing on Jesus, *truly* dwelling deep in His Word, then we will fall in love with Him. Both as an overflow of our love and in direct response to His command, the natural result of this love will be a desire deep down in our souls to obey and serve Him and to tell others about Him. These desires won't be something you should have to *strive* to do. They should be as natural as breathing. If a person has no desire to serve the Lord and His people, he may need to examine whether or not he is really dwelling deep in God's Word and falling more in love with Him day by day.

A person can be in ten Bible studies a week, reading three chapters of the Bible a day, attending church every time the doors are open, and still not be growing in love with the Savior. One test of love is the desire to obey.

But lest I make it sound too simple, there are some steps we can take to ensure that we are obeying. One friend of mine has a unique way of heeding the Word of God, which he calls "immediate obedience."

"If I'm reading the Bible," he says, "and it tells me, 'Sing a new song unto the Lord,' I do just that—even if I have to make up the song. Or, if the Lord says, 'Love your neighbor,' at the first available opportunity I go out and do an act of love for my neighbor. That's 'immediate obedience.'"

If we all lived in this kind of obedience—when the Lord speaks, we act—not only would our faith be kept fresh, but outreach to others would be a natural thing that happens in the process every day.

Yet, so many of us think, "What can I do?" The answer is, "Whatever God asks me to." Examples abound.

My mother-in-law is ninety-two, and to this day she

continues to have an outreach. She prays two hours a day for women around the world. Another person I know has a letter outreach to prisoners. It's not really a matter of asking, "What can I do?" but instead responding, "Yes, Lord. Show me what you want me to do."

One time at a book convention, I met the dearest old lady—she was probably eighty-five years old. Her eyes sparkled as she told me how she had been widowed for twenty years. Her husband had left her with enough money to live comfortably, so she thought about what she would do with her life. She said, "I could sit with other old ladies and rock my life away. I could get involved in community projects and play bridge each week. Or I could give the rest of my life to God. I decided that's what I'd do."

Since then this lady has been to Vietnam to hand out refugee packages. She has been to Papua New Guinea and had arrows shot over her head from wild tribesmen. She has been kicked out of Colombia for preaching against communism.

Her face literally shone—as does my mother-in-law's—with a light from within. Those people have fallen in love with Jesus and couldn't *not* share their Beloved!

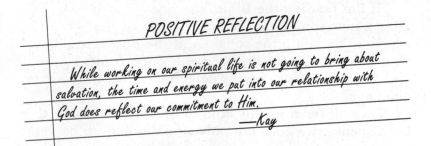

POSITIVE REFLECTION

While working on our spiritual life is not going to bring about salvation, the time and energy we put into our relationship with God does reflect our commitment to Him.

—Kay

Faith is not just about knowing I'm saved. It's about obeying and serving the One I love, which will result in sharing my knowledge and freedom with others. If I'm reluctant—if I refuse—to obey in serving and sharing, I need to examine my love to see if it's lukewarm or even dead. And remember James 2:26, which says, ". . . faith without deeds is dead."

Out On a Limb

The third key to keeping my faith fresh is courage. My faith grows and becomes vital when I put myself out on a limb with God. Jack and I learned about the importance of courage when we lived in Portland, Oregon.

We had gotten ourselves into debt—a situation we felt displeased God. We prayed for Him to furnish the lump sum, several hundred dollars, that we needed to clear our debts, but He didn't answer that prayer. Finally we said, "All right, Lord, what is it you want?"

Ultimately, we felt Him leading us to pay all our bills at the beginning of each month, which left us with no money for food or anything else until Jack's next monthly paycheck. I'll admit, following God's directive was scary. Though my faith felt small, we obeyed God in confidence that He would fulfill His promises.

Unfortunately, most of us don't look at God that way. We say we believe He is who He says He is, yet we have our plan B in place just in case He doesn't come through. When Jack and I stepped out in faith with our financial situation, we confessed it was our fault we were in debt, and together we determined to trust God completely to meet our needs. In a sense, we put ourselves out on a limb for God. And if that limb collapsed, so would our faith.

But God is rock solid. We didn't tell a soul about our needs, and, in the six months that followed, tremendous things happened. Jack found a wallet full of money during this time. We returned it to the owner, who was so astounded he gave us a reward. A week later, we found a bag of groceries on our back porch—anonymously donated.

During this time, Jack had an emergency appendectomy and we did not have one cent of insurance. The day the hospital bill came, three different men in the church, without knowing of our need, gave Jack money that was enough to pay the hospital bill. The day the doctor bill came, a tax refund arrived and covered the entire bill.

For six months, until the debt was erased, God supplied for us in miraculous ways. I often pray God will not allow me to get comfortable and do only those things I think I can handle. In many situations I say, "Lord, what have you gotten us into this time?" Then the Lord quietly says, "Carole, nothing that I can't handle."

There's no question it is frightening to go out on a limb. But so often we keep ourselves in a comfortable spot and say, "I couldn't do that," when all the while God is prompting us, saying, "Give it a try." As the noted missionary Jim Elliot once said, "God's will is always bigger than we bargain for."

Revived and Renewed

If your faith lacks a freshness, if your heart doesn't seem to be in it, Psalm 19:7 is a valuable reminder of what the Lord has planned for us, "The law of the Lord is perfect, reviving the soul." God's Word will revive us, it will keep us fresh.

A few years ago, when Jack was on an extended trip overseas, I learned just how God's Word can revive us. One night I was so lonely I couldn't sleep. I decided to try meditating on the Psalms, but when I read the first one, it didn't speak to my heart. Then I skipped to Psalm 36. As I read the words, vivid images began to fill my mind. "They feast on the abundance of your house; you give them drink from your river of delights" (v. 8).

I pictured myself sitting at the edge of the beautiful, wide, and flowing river of God's delights with a demitasse cup. Being very thirsty, I filled my cup and took a sip. It was so wonderful, I took another cupful. I then looked up to see the Lord at the mouth of this river. Then I could see God smiling as He said, "Carole, here's a ten-gallon bucket. Fill it and drink up. Better yet, why don't you jump right in and let my river flow all over you."

As I thought about that verse I realized that I am content with so little when God wants to give me so much. And by dwelling richly in His Word, I caught a glimpse of how much God gives.

When you ask God for those daily delights and insights from His Word, it's as if He taps you on the shoulder and says, "This is just for you today." It is this intimacy and understanding that revives us spiritually. And if we continue to dwell richly in the Word and drink deeply, we can be confident that very soon God will do something special to renew our faith.

Make It Happen

1. Practice uncluttering your mind by spending five minutes scribbling as fast as you can all the stray thoughts zooming through your mind. Don't worry if you can't read the words. Just scribble notes. At the end of five minutes, crumple up the paper and toss it aside. Now open your Bible and focus on what God specifically wants to share with you. If more stray thoughts return, grab another piece of paper and spend one minute putting them down. After a minute is up, return to your Bible.

2. For one week practice "immediate obedience." Put what you've read in your Bible each day in action at the first possible opportunity.

3. If your faith seems a bit stale, ask a friend how God has been active in her life. What special insights and blessings has she experienced in the past week? Don't compare, but rather look at it as a time to rejoice and be encouraged by the wonderful ways God works.

4. Do a mini-inventory of your outreach. What new knowledge about the Lord have you gained in the past week? How has that new knowledge gone beyond your head and into your heart and actions?

Survival Tips for Spiritual Blahs

Pamela Hoover Heim

Lucy Pemberton, a fellow student at Denver Seminary, once said, "Sometimes the Christian life is like shredded wheat. It's dry, but it's good for you." Imagine that! Dryness is not something to lament or question. If it is not caused by sin, then it can be good for us. What are some of the benefits of a winter season of the soul?

Feeling lonely for God prompts us to come to Him. I believe what hunger is to eating and thirst is to drinking, spiritual homesickness is to intimacy with God.

When we feel uneasy, we tend to reevaluate our relationship to God and give it more attention. It's good to take stock of our spiritual life when God seems distant, but we need to remember that He is the one who takes the initiative to point out if we are off course.

Dry times force us to live not by sight but by faith. When the disciple Thomas demanded that Jesus prove His resurrection to him, our Savior said, "Because you have seen me, you have believed; blessed are those who have not seen and yet have believed" (John 20:29). Jesus sees faith that doesn't depend on constant validation as blessed and mature.

Feeling far from God often helps us correct some wrong assumptions about who He is and how He relates to His children. After speaking at a retreat and sharing some rough times I was facing, a woman told me I could have a problem-free life and still feel God was so close I could reach out and touch Him. The problem was, the way she saw God—concerned about making our lives safe and happy—simply isn't biblical.

Our relationship with God is not a matter of figuring out how

63

to "work" Him to get the desired emotional payback. Ours is a personal relationship with Him to cling to when we feel better or worse, richer or poorer, in sickness or in health.

—From *Today's Christian Woman* (July/August 1991)

5

How Can I Know God's Will for My Life?

—Carole Mayhall

IF WE HOPE TO UNDERSTAND and follow God's will, it's helpful to realize it consists of two distinct, but related, aspects. First, there is His revealed will for all believers—the manner in which He desires us to live. Second is God's specific will for many choices that face us in life. For example, should I take this new job or not?

God's revealed will is clearly stated throughout Scripture. For instance, 1 Thessalonians 4:3–4 says, "It is God's will that you should be sanctified: that you should avoid sexual immorality; that each of you should learn to control his own body in a way that is holy and honorable." Another example of God's revealed will is in Ephesians 5:17, "Therefore do not be foolish, but understand what the Lord's will is." The passage goes on to talk about not being drunk with wine but being filled by the Spirit and the need to speak to one another with psalms, hymns, and spiritual songs.

Before we can address the questions we have about God's specific will, we must look at how we are leading our lives in light of His revealed will. Take God's command that we walk in love. If, after a tough day, I snap at my family and take out my frustration on them in a hateful way, I'm obviously not living in God's will.

In situations like this we don't even need to ask God to show us His will. We simply need to have an understanding of what Scripture teaches us about holy living.

If I'm not obeying the revealed will of God, it isn't likely that I will receive further instruction on the specific choices I face in my life. That would be like asking for directions when I hold a road map in my hands. More than likely, the person I ask will say, "Read your map. My directions would only add to your confusion."

A Fork in the Road

Once we've made a concentrated effort to know and follow God's revealed will, we can ask for His direction on the specifics in our life—those forks in the road. At some point or another, we all wrestle with knowing God's specific will. What college should I go to? Whom should I marry? Should I go back to work after my baby is born? On such major life issues, we want to know God's will.

Fortunately, we can relax a little on knowing God's specific will for one simple reason—one many of us overlook. Discerning God's specific will is not a mystery game where He's trying to hold something back from us. Often we feel we must go through layers and layers, all the time wondering, "Will God really let me know about this?" when all along God is saying, "Hey, I'll show you." He is a God who loves us and *wants* us to find His will. We can be confident He will give us the light we need to see His will for us. We just need to have an open heart to His leading.

I find it useful to keep in mind that God is the perfect parent. For instance, let's say my son or daughter comes and asks me for advice about the suitability of a nonbeliever as a spouse. If I know from experience that this relationship will lead to problems yet I withhold my advice, what kind of parent would I be? A good parent will wait until she is asked for advice and then she will freely share her concerns and guidance out of love.

BE SENSIBLE

Do you really want to know God's will? If the answer to that question is "yes," know that God is on your side! He is far more eager for us to discover His will than we are to seek it. Be in the Scriptures—developing your prayer life. Be sensible not mystical. God's will is usually the next sensible thing I need to do!

—Jill

In the same way, God gives us direction in our life if we ask for it. But many times preconceived notions of what we think God's will for our life is prevents us from being open to His direction. If we hope to find and follow God's will on the specifics, we need to forgo these preconceived ideas.

I know of a woman who was certain God wanted her to be a missionary. She did everything in her power to make this happen. She even went to the mission site after her funding fell through. Consequently, she had a less than positive experience. She continued to persist with the idea of missions work to the point where her health began to deteriorate under the stress. Throughout this period she never felt that sense of peace that affirms our choices. God was directing her toward another career, but she wasn't open to it.

A Word for Us

God directs in many ways—sometimes with absolute clarity, other times He seems obscure and vague. One method God uses to show us His will is through His Word. When Jack and I were young in our Christian lives, most of the time God made His direction known to us in precise and clear ways. A passage of Scripture would leap out from the page and pull at our hearts.

Jack and I had been in Portland for just over a year when one day, as I was reading in Deuteronomy, the Lord seemed to stop me at one particular verse, "See, the LORD your God has given you the land. Go up and take possession of it as the LORD, the God of your fathers, told you. Do not be afraid; do not be discouraged" (1:21).

As I tried to read on, over and over I was pulled back to that one verse. "Oh, no," I said to myself. "I love it here in Portland and we haven't been here all that long. God certainly wouldn't want us to go to some 'new land!' " But there was a "stop and take note" command to my spirit again and again. I tried to ignore it but thought I'd better be prepared and willing if God had plans for us to move. Finally, after a struggle, I said to the Lord, "All right, Father! I hope I'm not hearing this right, but if you want us to go to a 'new land,' then I'm willing."

Less than six months later we had moved to a new part of the country and begun a new job and ministry. And I didn't even *argue* with Jack when he felt it was God's will because God had already told me!

A couple of years later, we were asked to move to the Chicago area and begin a ministry with university students. Our suggestions of how to support ourselves while doing so were all turned down as the leadership felt that our time would be more than filled with the opportunities of ministry. So the bottom line was for us to move and trust God for the finances.

Such a step in faith was scary to say the least, and I felt that I needed God's promise and assurance that this was what we should do. The Lord had given Jack some direction on this, but I wanted my own promise and direction. God gave it to me in 2 Corinthians 9:10, "Now he who supplies seed to the sower and bread for food will also supply and increase your store of seed and will enlarge the harvest of your righteousness." How amazing and wonderful God is! He not only gave me a promise for our physical needs (bread for food), but for the blessing of the ministry (a harvest of righteousness).

I needed that very concrete promise and direction because our faith was frequently tested in those months following our move. I often meditated on a phrase from a sermon I once heard, "Never doubt in the dark what God has shown you in the light." If I hadn't found God's will in the light—from his Word—I don't think I would have made it through the next year.

———— ✍ ————

As we have grown older, these specific and concrete ways of discerning God's will have diminished. Not always does a verse leap out at me or a friend offer unexpected biblical counsel on a tough decision I'm facing.

Why does this happen? Drawing parallels to my own marriage helps clarify the answer. When I first married Jack, I had to ask him about everything. How do you like your coffee? How do you take your steak? What kind of music do you like? Do you like to sleep with the windows open?

I needed to ask all these questions because I didn't know Jack. Today, after more than forty years of marriage, rarely do questions like this come up. I've lived with Jack long enough to know the answers, and, to a certain degree, anticipate his answers. I know what to do because I know Jack.

The same is true with the Lord. When you have walked with God for some time, you begin to know what He wants. You don't have to ask as many questions about what you should or shouldn't do. Now, for me, the way I sense God's leading on decisions is more like a nudge. With gentle promptings, I become aware of which speaking engagements to accept or what projects

I should take on. A quieter leading has replaced the momentous signs of what God wants me to do.

Peace That Passes Understanding

Another way we can be assured the choices we make are in accordance with God's will is by having a sense of peace that truly surpasses all understanding.

Jack and I experienced this peace as we took the steps that led us to where we are now in our ministry. After finishing seminary, Jack accepted a job at a church. Soon, though, we felt God leading him to resign from that position. At the same time, a fantastic ministry opportunity lay before us. We were sure it was God's will for us to pursue this, but we continued to pray together for direction. In fact, Jack gave it a tremendous amount of prayer. Although the circumstances seemed to point us in the direction of choosing that job, there was a hesitation in Jack's spirit about the position. A great unrest of sorts—much like 1 Corinthians 14:33, which says, "For God is not a God of disorder but of peace." Jack simply didn't have any peace about the job, but instead confusion. So, without knowing why, we turned down the offer.

Even without a job in the immediate future, Jack went through with his resignation at the church, convinced God had something in store for us. For four months he was without a job. I went through all sorts of questioning during that time. Did we do the right thing? Did we hear God wrong? This was a tough period for us, both financially and emotionally. But God taught us so much while we waited.

He showed me that when I become anxious, certain God has put us away on some high shelf, I have to stop praying about the situation and instead pray about my heart, that it might be changed, because Philippians 4:6 (NASB) commands me to, "Be anxious for *nothing*" (italics added). I needed to learn to give my anxiety over to the Lord.

Finally, God answered our prayers and opened up the job in Portland, where Jack became both youth director and assistant pastor. Looking back, we realized if God had not stopped us by putting a sense of unrest in Jack's heart, we'd be in an entirely different field than we are now.

———— ⟨∞⟩ ————

God led us then, and He still does today, as we make decisions in our lives. And God gives us His peace apart from circumstances, which is a critical point to remember. It would have been easy for Jack and me to look at the ministry opportunity that presented itself immediately after he resigned from his first church position and assume that God had worked out the circumstances in our favor. Yet neither Jack nor I had that sense of peace about the decision. Had we overlooked this significant factor in the decision-making process, we would have chosen the wrong course. Experience has shown me that circumstances should be low on the list of determining if a choice is within God's will or not.

If, however, circumstances fall in line with other directives like a clear message from Scripture or a sense of peace, they can be a great affirmation in following God's will. But many times God leads us totally apart from circumstances, and we need to be aware of that. We can be blinded if we operate solely by circumstances.

Can We Miss the Path?

What if we unintentionally make the wrong choice? That's possible, I'm sure. We are confronted daily with decisions, and sometimes we overlook the signs that point us in a particular direction.

But I don't think we should be greatly concerned about missing God's will. We don't have to fear that any more than a child running around in a huge field has to worry about falling into a crevice or being attacked by wolves. Under the watchful eye of a concerned parent, that child is protected from life-threatening dangers.

Remember, God is our perfect parent. If we are willing to do His will and our hearts are eager to obey Him, we need not be concerned with unintentionally making a wrong choice. We may fall and stub our toe, but our Father will protect us from major error.

HE WILL LEAD YOU

If I have presented my body to Christ as a living sacrifice, desiring only what He wants, and if my mind is being renewed in God's Word, He will show me His will and it will be good, acceptable and perfect (see Romans 12:1–2).

—Kay

It's the intentional choices we'd better be concerned about—the decisions we make without asking Him, the judgments we execute knowing they are contrary to His will.

God doesn't want us to make mistakes. However, He does give us the ultimate freedom as to whether we will heed His guidance or not. We have the option to choose what we know is *not* God's will.

For instance, if I make the deliberate choice, against the knowledge and counsel of God's Word and others, to marry a non-Christian, I need to realize what the consequences of my choice will be, knowing that Galatians 6:7 says, "A man reaps what he sows. The one who sows to please his sinful nature, from that nature will reap destruction; the one who sows to please the Spirit, from the Spirit will reap eternal life."

I will live with the consequences of my wrong choice. However, the other side of the coin is that the moment I ask for forgiveness for that sin, I am again in God's will. God can take that situation and weave that painful black thread into a tapestry that will glorify Him. The story of Joseph and his brothers proves that. Joseph's brothers deliberately sinned in selling Joseph into slavery. Yet God used that terrible choice not only to give direction to Joseph's life, but to deliver his whole family—including his brothers—from famine. And when Joseph's brothers wept in repentance, Joseph replied, "You intended to harm me, but God intended it for good to accomplish what is now being done, the saving of many lives" (Genesis 50:20).

———— ✑ ————

God's revealed will for us never changes. He always wants us to walk in love, to avoid sin, and to praise Him continually. On the other hand, His specific will for our lives will continue to be revealed to us each day. And as we discern and follow His will, we can have confidence that it is a loving, caring Father who is leading us in a certain direction.

Make It Happen

1. Be open to how God can make His will known. It can be through His Word, through the unasked counsel of a friend, or a sense of inner peace. Learn to be open to how God can get His message through. Remember, He is wonderfully creative. We just need to have receptive and open hearts.

2. Proverbs 16:9 reads, "In his heart a man plans his course, but the LORD determines his steps." Consider keeping a journal of those "big" questions you need to

ask God for specific direction. Then, as He makes His direction known, make a note of it. How often was God's direction different from what you anticipated?

3. As you try to learn God's specific will for your life, learn to relax. Remember, just as important as finding and following God's will is the need to have a vital and growing relationship with Him. From this relationship will come the answers you need to follow His will—both revealed and specific. Psalm 36:9 clearly spells out this truth: "In your light we see light." It is in His light that we see what to do. But if we are not allowing His light to shine on our lives, we can expect to roam around in the dark.

6

How Can a Busy Woman Maintain Her Spiritual Life?

—*Jill Briscoe*

WOMEN TODAY ARE NOT nearly as busy as women have been down through the ages.

"Now wait a minute," you might say. "I've read about how stressed out we are, how demanding our daily schedules are." Yes, but if we look at history, my statement isn't nearly as surprising as it seems—we *aren't* as busy as we think.

It wasn't until the middle of this century that women had the option to stay home and focus their energy on one job—homemaking. Until then, the majority of women worked outside the home—it might have been in the field or in the family shop, but they worked. Consider the women in Jesus' time. They worked in the fields all day, then returned home to even more work as mother, wife, and servant. Or look at the women in Third World cultures. They gather water from the well, find the wood to chop for the fire, and grind the flour to make bread. Their day may include a five-mile walk to the nearest market. I don't think we really know what busy means.

For many of us in our modern Western culture, ours is so often a self-imposed busyness. The single mother who holds down two jobs to support her kids might be an exception, but the rest of us have simply added and added to our daily schedules until we can't squeeze in another activity.

Strangely, I've noted that those women who complain most about their busy schedules and say they find it difficult to find time for God, in reality don't *have* to be so busy. Do you ever find yourself overcommitted? It's easy to say "yes" to people. We sometimes agree to do something for fear we'll be disliked if we say "no." Or possibly the one asking is intimidating and, before we know it, one more activity has been added to a packed calendar. We'd like to kick ourselves for saying "yes," for being pushed into something we really don't need to be doing.

God, however, does not seem as concrete or intimidating as the flesh-and-blood asker towering over us! It's somehow easier to say "yes" to a person and "no" to God than the other way around.

If your busyness is self-imposed and hinders your time with God, then stop and ask yourself, "Do I have to be so busy? How can I simplify my life? If I say 'no' to this activity will that make space for God?" It's a huge challenge to say "no" to those things that aren't a necessity, but that's what we must do.

Besides, I've noticed that those women who are over-busy out of necessity are more open to finding time for God despite the schedule crunch. While staying in many a home on the mission fields of this world, I have observed dedicated and over-extended Bible teachers and physicians who have schedules that make our busiest days look like a vacation. Yet, I've seen these men and women resolutely rise an hour before duty time to meet with God. And this is when duty calls at 6:00 A.M.!

———— ❧ ————

If we hope to have a growing faith despite a busy schedule we first need to turn to the principles that make the spiritual life work—truths that can't be broken. Unfortunately, we often want to bypass these principles and immediately go to the end result. We desire a growing and close relationship with the Lord—only that can't happen unless we obey the principles. Both Stuart and I doggedly teach principles. At the end of a sermon or talk, we take time to restate the principles that are necessary for a spiritual life to succeed. For instance, after one of my husband's sermons, I talked with a girl who told me she had no peace of mind. "I want it so badly," she said. "How can I recover that peace I once knew when I first came to Christ?"

Knowing her circumstances, I replied without hesitation, "Move out of your boyfriend's apartment."

"That has nothing to do with peace," she shot back.

She wanted the peace of a clear conscience without obedience to a biblical principle—that of sexual integrity before marriage. It doesn't work that way.

If we hope to find time for God we must hold to two essential principles. The first is that despite a crammed schedule and hundreds of responsibilities *we need to make a conscious decision that we will have a vital relationship with the Lord.* It's much like making a covenant, of saying to the Lord, "I am going to keep close to you." The second principle is that *we must commit to spending time with Him.* You can't hope to develop an intimate relationship with Christ unless you make time for Him in your life.

These two principles are foundational to our growth in the Lord, the basis on which all of our spiritual activities should rest. It's up to us as individuals to work out the practicalities of implementing these principles. No one else can do it for us.

To make these principles a reality, start by asking yourself, "When will I find one-on-one time with the Lord?" "How will I spend it?" "How much time do I need?" Factors like whether or not you are married, the number of children you have, their ages, and if you work outside the home will all play into the way you choose to live out your commitment to spiritual growth.

GOD OF THE DAILIES

Early in my married life, I discovered I didn't see God as a God of the daily in my life. And my life was so daily. Back then, if I didn't see Him operating on a miracle level, I would get bored. Not until I began to talk to God about all the little things in my life did my faith take on an exciting new dimension.
—Carole

Since no two women are alike, there are no easy answers or simple formulas. Books and magazine articles can give you ideas and insights, but since we are all unique and different, what works for the author may not work for you.

You have to meet with God when it is a good time for you—not when someone tells you it's time to meet with Him. The only way you'll find that time is to know yourself, your schedule, your lifestyle and your personal preferences. The best thing to do is start somewhere—anywhere—but start! Don't spend hours getting ready for it and end up with no time to do it! Start before work and see if that time works out. Or try during a nap-time break if you have small children at home. Make mid-course corrections. As your life changes, make adjustments.

——— ✆ ———

Once you've committed yourself to the two principles—a vital relationship with God and one-on-one time with Him—the next step is to capture that time. Don't just say you'll do it. Take the calendar off the wall and write down when you're going to spend time with the Lord. It may vary from day to day—it may be right after breakfast one morning or right before dinner the next day. Find the best time Monday through Friday *this week* and put it on your calendar just as you would jot down a dentist appointment, a lunch date with friends, or a game of tennis.

If we hope to achieve the goal of our spiritual life—a growing relationship with the Lord—we've got to start with the principles and work down to the details. It can't happen the other way around. Principles are the "why"; practicals are the "what." The Lord says in Psalm 46:10, "Be still, and know that I am God." I need to meet with Him not because it's a nice idea or makes me feel good, but because God tells me in His Word that it is an essential discipline if I am to fulfill His goal for my life—Christlikeness. I cannot be like Jesus without abiding in His presence.

These principles are taught in God's Word. If we start by saying, "What shall I do in my quiet time," instead of "Why should I have a quiet time," we will quit when we get busy or bored. If we have our quiet time starting with any other premise than this—a quiet time is God's desire for us—then our attempts will fail.

————— ❧ —————

Some years ago, there was a woman who was intensely active in our church. She headed up the women's ministry and participated in several Bible studies. At the same time, though, her family life was suffering because of her over-involvement at church. I finally told her I thought it might be in her best interest to cut back on church activities until she could get her family on track.

Initially, her response was, "How will I ever grow spiritually without my women's ministry?"

And I said, "You will grow with the Lord better on your own than you ever did with everybody else."

It was almost a year before she resumed her involvement in several of the church programs. But while she was away she made significant strides spiritually. While corporate experiences of fellowship, worship, and study are vital to our spiritual growth, as this one woman discovered, our times in corporate activities can be a holy substitute.

I see this happening quite a bit on Christian college campuses. There is so much offered spiritually that students find it more "fun" to go to three Bible studies a week with their peers than to shut themselves in their rooms for some one-on-one time with God.

If you take your food secondhand, it has been chewed by someone else before it gets to you. To take your food from the hand of the Giver is always the biggest blessing.

Super Stretch

As busy women, we shouldn't be concerned with simply *maintaining* our spiritual life—we need to see it mature as well. We can, if we so choose, reach a plateau in our spiritual development and comfortably stay there. However, we would then miss the opportunity to go to newer and higher levels of understanding and growth.

In my travels, I've met a few women who teach other women in the church, yet they have confided to me that their personal time with the Lord is virtually non-existent. They have learned to operate at a certain level with a polished talk they've done hundreds of times. Frankly, when you get stuck in a rut like this you're not even open to God's help.

If we were honest we would admit it, as General Campbell Morgan once did when he feared God saying to him, "Preach on, great preacher, without me." He realized that it is possible to be biblically accurate, verbally fluent, and theologically profound, yet spiritually useless.

One thing that will keep your spiritual life vital is, when you are on risk's edge, to be willing to do what is unfamiliar. The majority of the gifts I practice—speaking, teaching, and putting together multi-media presentations—I perform reasonably well. So unless I force myself to venture into uncharted territory and accept new challenges each year, my faith begins to stagnate.

Most recently, my opportunity to stretch came in the form of serving on the board of World Relief. By nature I'm an artistic, reflective person—not the type who would jump at a chance to serve on a board. However, I was finally persuaded by the president of the relief organization to serve as vice-president. But I did so only after he promised me two things—he would never be sick or die! If either of those two things happened, I'd be responsible for leading the board meetings—something that terrified me, because I had never led a formal board meeting in my life.

The president stuck to his word for eighteen months. Then a friend died and he needed to attend the funeral. He explained this in a call to me the night before a major board meeting. He wanted me to lead the meeting. My initial impulse was to see if another board member could do the job. But the president insisted I do it, so I accepted the challenge knowing only God could get me through the experience.

I went to bed at midnight, only to awaken frantic at 3:00 A.M. I had the agenda but no time to prepare—let alone learn parliamentary procedure. I spent a long time memorizing the agenda, carefully writing out what to say when.

I arrived at the meeting, confident I would know what to do as long as we followed the agenda. I promptly learned the agenda had been scrapped and was given a revised agenda with arrows pointing every which way for what should be first, what should be second. On top of that, several board members were upset about an issue and needed to be placated.

There was no doubt, I was on risk's edge. Thankfully, the skills I had used to calm angry members at past women's meetings transferred well to this setting.

Though it was a horrendous experience for me, the men on the board were very helpful and accommodating. I realized that God keeps us afloat even when it feels like we've never learned to swim but have been thrown out into the deep end. And turning to God in my need revitalized my faith and trust in Him.

Find a Fit

As we seek to mature in our spiritual life, I can't stress enough how important it is first to begin with the principles of a covenant to know God and a willingness to spend time with Him—one-on-one time. Don't be discouraged when your schedule doesn't permit you to join a 9:00 A.M. weekday Bible study for mothers because it falls on a day you work. Don't think your spiritual life has to follow the blueprint of a close friend or the author of a successful book. Instead, look for those opportunities that will mesh with your unique schedule and needs as you attempt to incorporate these two vital principles into your life.

SETTING PRIORITIES

Don't let anyone put you under the Law by saying, "If you really love Jesus, you'll teach Sunday school, be involved in the women's ministries, or be in church every time the doors are open." If you really love Jesus, you'll do what He wants you to do, which may be to devote yourself first and foremost to your family. Remember, husbands and children are eternal beings who not only need to hear the Gospel, but need to be nurtured in it through exposure to a consecrated life born out of genuine intimacy with the Father.

—Kay

A busy life is no excuse for allowing our relationship with God to take low priority among all the demands on our time. Today, we are so organized, so programmed to learn about God, that we often forget to meet with the God we are learning about. He wants us to stretch and grow each day with Him.

Make It Happen

1. Spend some time in a Christian bookstore looking over the wide variety of devotional materials available that can supplement your Bible reading. Find one that works best for you. Do you like to read a little each day? Do you like to reflect and write your thoughts out? Do you prefer the insights of noted authors and speakers? Select the best ideas or materials with the goal of creating a quiet time that is unique and as individual as you.

2. Are you too busy to be blessed? Remember Martha who was "cumbered by much serving," and Mary who "hath chosen the better part, which shall not be taken away from her" (Luke 10:40–42, KJV) by spending time at the Lord's feet. At the end of each day, look back at how you spent your hours. How often could you identify with Martha? How often with Mary? Make it a goal to identify with Mary more than Martha.

3. Look for the "stretch" experiences God places before you. Are you afraid to try something because it isn't comfortable, it isn't familiar? As you see these opportunities arise, bring them before the Lord with an open heart and ask for His continued direction. If all signs are go, stretch yourself. Do so with the confidence that it is God who wants you to stretch for a purpose you may not immediately see.

Where Do I Find the Time?
Denise Turner

Today's busy woman frequently struggles to find time for daily Bible study. But here are some tips to help you strategize time for studying God's Word.

Ask yourself why you have trouble finding time. Be honest: Is it lack of time, or is something else involved? Many people put Bible study last on their day's agenda, then never get to it because they're tired or uninspired. If this is the case, acknowledge the problem.

Shop around for Bible study books you enjoy. Whether you like a light, personal approach or a more scholarly one, you'll find a wide selection at your local Christian bookstore.

Set aside a specific place and time for Bible study. Human beings are creatures of habit. Find a time when you are energetic and alert, then arrange your schedule accordingly.

Think of your Bible study time as a natural stress reducer. Tell your family you need time alone every day so you can study the Bible.

If you are people-oriented, plan Bible study time with your husband or a friend. Combine this with a workout or a neighborhood stroll before or after study to improve your physical and spiritual health.

Spot the time wasters in your life, like TV, clutter, even worry. Set out to organize your time by streamlining your life.

Lastly, set priorities. If you get off track, approach Bible study like a diet and get right back on. And, like a diet, with discipline your goal can be reached.

—From *Today's Christian Woman* (March/April 1989)

PART TWO

UNDERSTANDING MY DOUBTS

AS CHRISTIANS we'll always be joyful. We'll always feel loved by God and in intimate fellowship with Him. Bible reading and daily devotional time will always come naturally. It will be a breeze to fit the disciplines of a "good" Christian life into our packed schedule.

Wouldn't it be nice if at the moment we accepted Christ our life turned into a series of absolutes, and the road to spiritual maturity involved nothing more than following an easy-to-read map.

But the road to spiritual maturity isn't easy. Along the way, we will have our doubts and our uncertainties—not to mention our share of frustrations.

How do we clear the slate of mistaken assumptions and unrealistic expectations that can cast gray clouds on our spiritual walk?

In this section Kay, Jill, and Carole look at the sources of our expectations and examine those nagging questions like, "Where is the joy I expected?" "Why is life so painful?" or "Why can't I forgive?" in hopes of showing how we can use our doubts and frustrations as opportunities for spiritual growth rather than harbingers of spiritual burn-out.

7
Why Don't the Disciplines of the Spiritual Life Come Easy?

—*Carole Mayhall*

THE IDEA THAT the Christian walk will be an easy one certainly doesn't come from the Bible. Yet, somehow we think once we've accepted Christ all the disciplines of the spiritual life will fall into place without too much effort.

Throughout the Scriptures, never do we hear that discipleship is effortless. Just look at the commands God gives us and expects us to follow. For instance, the kind of love Jesus commands, as described in Matthew 10:37–38, is anything but easy. The Lord says, "Anyone who loves his father or mother more than me is not worthy of me; anyone who loves his son or daughter more than me is not worthy of me; and anyone who does not take his cross and follow me is not worthy of me."

Those who long for a deep relationship with God, who pray for a hunger for Him and a thirst for His righteousness, know the Christian walk is anything but easy. Throughout my life, I've had to work hard at my spiritual life for the same reason I work hard at any relationship—if I don't, it is going to weaken and grow stagnant. Working at a relationship doesn't mean spending a few minutes here and a few minutes there—it means investing my heart and mind in the relationship constantly.

Not long ago, Jack and I spoke at a marriage conference about the need to continually work at marriage for it to succeed. After we finished our presentation, a couple from the audience approached us and asked with genuine sincerity, "Say we have two hours to work on our marriage. What should we do?"

Jack and I exchanged glances. It was obvious what we had tried to communicate in our talk hadn't come through to this couple. We took a few minutes and sat down with them and reviewed what working on a relationship entailed.

We reminded them that working on a marriage is a twenty-four-hour-a-day job. It's not something you squeeze in when you have a few spare moments. And in each twenty-four-hour period, you have to resolve whatever differences crop up. That means being quick to ask for and offer forgiveness. It means serving each other unselfishly. And it means making time for each other a top priority.

BASIS FOR BUILDING

Finding out what spiritual disciplines work best for you comes through trial and error—but nothing will work if you don't first have a relationship with Christ.

—*Kay*

As we talked, I became aware of the tremendous number of similarities between a relationship with a spouse and our relationship with God. If we apply the same basic disciplines to our Christian life that are required of a marriage relationship, we gain a deep intimacy with the Lord. And just as our love for a spouse becomes more firmly rooted by investing time and energy into the relationship, so too do we grow with Christ when we work at our spiritual life.

While a relationship does take an investment of time to develop, it's important that we realize it is work that makes it succeed, not *works*. For years it was difficult for me to distinguish between "work" and "works."

Shortly after my father died, I found myself having absolutely no sense of the presence of God. I was doing all the right things—I led two Bible studies, I was involved in person-to-person discipleship, I memorized Scripture. But still I didn't feel God in my life. For three or four months all I could think was, "Carole, you hypocrite. Here you are in full-time Christian work, and you're not even sure any of it is real." I would pray and pray and pray, but nothing changed until I read a little book by Roy Hession called *We Would See Jesus* (Christian Literature Crusade). What he said was the key that opened the door in my spiritual life. With this book, two insights gradually became clear to me.

The first was that I was in the habit of coming to God *for something*—a blessing, a sense of peace, or for joy. Although I didn't hear Him at first, I sensed God saying, "I just want you." He let me get away with what I was doing—He still gave me those Wondrous Things each day—but it became clear what He truly wanted was for me to come to Him just for Himself.

It's much like having a five-year-old come to you and preface each request with something she knows I want to hear. I'm not surprised to hear a child at age five say, "I love you, Mommy. Can I have a cookie?" But as a child grows older, a statement like, "I love you, Mom. Can I have $25?" makes me wonder, *Where is the relationship?* It certainly doesn't seem sincere and genuine when "I love you" is always couched with a request for something.

The second insight I gained from *We Would See Jesus*

was that I had been using spiritual disciplines, like Bible study and prayer, as a way to get to God—a way to know Him better and have more of His presence. Hession's book reminded me that *Jesus* is the only way to the Father. When Jesus dwells in me, as He has since I received Him, I have all of Him—His total self. The disciplines I use—studying the Bible, spending time in prayer as an expression of my love for Christ—may help me know Him better and mature in my relationship with Him, but I can never "earn" more of His presence or cause Him to love me more because He loves me *totally* this very moment.

Three Deadly Forces

At times we feel guilt when we don't meet our personal expectations for our spiritual life—our prayers seem haphazard, our Bible study only skims the surface. Sometimes the guilt is legitimate—we really have failed to invest any effort in the relationship. But there is another more prevalent force trying to sabotage our relationship with Christ: Satan.

Satan does what he can to draw us away from the Lord, and he uses three methods to do the job: the pressures of the world, our own human nature, and, finally, his direct attacks that come in a number of different forms. We are in a spiritual battle when it comes to our Christian life—never forget that.

———— ∽ ————

Most of us can attest to Satan's use of the pressures of this world to threaten our spiritual walk. He tries to press us into society's mold and defeat our relationships with our family and friends, as well as with the Lord.

One young mother looked at me with tears in her eyes and asked, "I've chosen to be a full-time mom these years that I have two preschoolers. But how do I keep from being bored to death?"

I blinked with surprise at her question and thought, *Bored to death with two little lives challenging you to creatively nurture them to grow to love Jesus? Bored to death with the struggle of being a helper for your husband? Bored to death with the call of serving the body of Christ in unique ways during these years you aren't working outside the home? How could you be bored?*

But then it hit me. The voices of the world around her had repeated the idea that being a full-time mother isn't living up to your full potential, is wasting your education, is not a worthy occupation. She had bought into that thinking to the point of *expecting* to be bored! Instead of realizing that being a mother is a call from God—a challenge and an adventure—she looked at it as a drag, as something to endure until she could go back to something more exciting.

Romans 12:2 says, in the Phillips version, "Don't let the world squeeze you into its own mold, but let God remold your minds from within, so that you may prove in practice that the plan of God for you is good, meets all his demands and moves towards the goal of true maturity."

The world has many ways of squeezing us into its mold. One primary way is by twisting our priorities out of whack. We are so success-oriented these days that we easily buy into the message of working longer hours at the expense of our families. Even "good" activities—church, school, community projects—can crowd our schedules as well, so that time for our husbands, our families, even for ourselves becomes a thing of the past.

It became evident as Jack and I talked with several husbands recently that the children were top priority in the lives of their wives. So much time was spent chauffeuring the children to anything and everything and then waiting for them that the husbands felt like low men on the totem pole. And the wives were unaware of the temptations this caused the husbands.

God has set up some biblical priorities for us, and the first two at the top are very clear: God himself (Matthew 6:33) and then our husbands (Titus 2:4–5). To the world, success often comes first, then our own needs, then friends or community involvement, and then, way down on the list, our families. God, of course, is left out entirely.

———— ✒ ————

Satan will also use our human weaknesses to pull us from the Lord. He will defeat us by our own "flesh," as the Bible calls it. One of my weaknesses is that I am sometimes just plain lazy.

The other night I felt very discouraged about several terrible problems that some of my friends were dealing with as well as my inability to help them with those hurts.

I was tired—tempted to just turn on the television or start reading a book to block out their problems and my own discouragement. My flesh was saying, "Forget it!" while my spirit was saying, "The thing you could do, Carole, is go to the Lord with the problem situations and with your own discouragement."

This time, instead of giving in to my lazy flesh, I forced myself to go up to my study and share with God my burden for my friends. Afterward, I was refreshed.

Battles of the flesh are fought every day. God says I must discipline my body, bring it under subjection and control my fleshly desires. But that takes work! It takes effort to pray instead of read the paper; it is a struggle to get up a few minutes early to be with God; it takes discipline to control a temper after a bad day; it is a chore to visit a nursing home when I want to go shopping. Satan will defeat me through my own nature if he can.

PULLED OFF COURSE

We are all born with a propensity to sin, with a weight in our hearts that pulls us off course. No matter how "straight" we may aim for perfection, sin pulls us off course. In the words of Paul, "what I want to do I do not do" (Romans 7:15) because "sin dwells in us." It is far easier to allow that "pull" to have its way than to resist it. If we hope to redress the pull and allow God to aim us on a straight course and keep us rolling along in the right direction, it takes disciplined attitudes and actions.

—Jill

Finally, we need to beware of Satan's direct attacks that take our minds away from what is pleasing to the Lord. For me, that means being aware of my thought life. I have a very active imagination and sometimes it gets me into trouble. For instance, I'll wake up with a little pain in my arm. The next thing I know I'm imagining myself at the doctor's office being told I have cancer. Before long, I'm planning my memorial service. Instead of meditating on the Lord or His Word, I'm focusing on unfounded fears.

For others, direct attacks can come in the form of excessive worry. I know of one woman who, when her husband is an hour late, goes into a worry-mode that practically renders her non-functional. She can't concentrate. She paces. By the time her husband arrives home she is a mess.

Satan has a multitude of methods at his disposal as well as demons at his command. We are seeing more evidence of his direct attack in our country today than ever before, with the onslaught of demonic worship, the occult, the cults, New Age mysticism, and mind-altering drugs. An awareness of both his tactics and how to do battle with him is especially imperative today.

What's Realistic?

While Satan wields his tools against my spiritual life every day, I can also be defeated in my desire for a thriving spiritual life simply by my own unrealistic expectations.

For years I've had an expectation of having a good self-image. I've read about it, listened to lectures, talked to people who said that I should "be" something in order to feel good about myself.

At long last, I've come to a couple of conclusions. Nothing in the Bible says that a self-love is to be desired. I know the argument about loving your neighbor as yourself, but I can't see that as the point to the Lord's command. I've finally concluded that it is okay *not* to have a great self-image. In fact, to spend a lot of time trying to achieve that goal is to focus again on *me*, rather than forgetting all about me and focusing on the Lord. My prayer then became the verse in John 3:30, "He must become greater; I must become less." The expectations I had of being self-assured and feeling good about myself caused me trouble and actually became a stumbling block in my spiritual life.

Unrealistic expectations will do this in a lot of areas. My expectation of spending a day in Bible study when I'm working eighty hours a week between home and my job may be so defeating that I don't study the Bible at all. My expectation of calling on my neighbors or entertaining a group from church each week when I'm trying to balance a husband, three children, and a Bible class one night a week will either set me up for a nervous or physical breakdown or cause me to give up everything extra I'm doing.

So how do we evaluate our expectations for our Christian lives to see if they are realistic? How do we determine if they are what God wants for us, or a matter of our own desires? I've found it helps to do four things.

First, ask God for His wisdom and expect an answer. Often I pray James 1:5, "If any of you lacks wisdom, he should ask God, who gives generously to all without finding fault, and it will be given to him." I remember a time a number of years ago when I was involved in three different Bible studies—one for intake, one with a group I was leading, and one with a new Christian. With a small daughter and Jack's needs, I felt I wasn't doing anything well! So I asked God for His wisdom but didn't see how I could possibly drop anything I was doing. God showed me how I could use the study I was taking for my own growth, simplify it for the group I was leading and simplify it even more for the new Christian. That meant doing only one study each week instead of three—but doing that one well. It was a lesson that helped many other times in my life.

Second, be a student of yourself. Years ago, before I started to study both my personality and gifts, I volunteered to organize a women's retreat, and it nearly did me in. My family, home, and Bible studies were neglected as I struggled to organize this retreat. The retreat was blessed, but I ended up a mess.

When I became a student of who I am and what my gifts are, I realized I'm not good at organization. When I looked around and found other women in the body of Christ who *loved* to organize, I decided never again to volunteer to run a retreat.

When we study ourselves we'll learn such things as whether or not we tend to overcommit, or whether we tend to get excited about something but don't follow through. We'll also discover such practical things as when we are most alert. Early on I heard that God deserves the best time of my day—but what *is* that for me? I've learned it is *not* the moment I pop out of bed.

Third, recognize the different seasons of your life and adjust your expectations for yourself to your season. A young mother may not be able to consistently devote the time she might like to prayer and Bible study and must realize, at that point in her life, ten focused minutes with the Lord will have to be sufficient.

Ruth Graham once mentioned that she kept the Book of Proverbs open on the kitchen counter, and each time she went past she'd read a proverb and think about it. You might even have a verse on the refrigerator door or above the kitchen sink that you can read throughout the day and meditate on. Give yourself the luxury of knowing it is okay for your devotions to be done in snatches rather than in uninterrupted periods. But do take the time to evaluate your personal expectations against the demands of the season of life you are in. Ask yourself, *Is it realistic to hope for thirty peaceful minutes at 7:30 in the morning when I'm trying to get the kids to school?*

Fourth, ask for the counsel of a wise friend or your spouse. Jack is a very organized person, and at the beginning of each year actually takes the time to write out the goals he has for his spiritual life. I'm not as organized or goal-oriented—I tend to keep my expectations in my head. But when we do make time to share our expectations, more than once Jack has said, "Honey, is what you're expecting ultimately going to detract from what is really on your heart?" He helps me weed out those unrealistic expectations.

———— ⌒ ————

It takes two to make a relationship work. Our perfect Father is always extending His love, care, and attention to us, and when we make the effort on our part, the relationship can be wonderfully rewarding. Our devotional life should be viewed as the time we set aside to be face to face with the Lord to work on our relationship with Him. It should be a time when nothing comes between us and Him, a time when we can center our thoughts and our day on Him—a time of true communion.

Make It Happen

1. Ephesians 5:15–16 reads, "Be very careful, then, how you live—not as unwise but as wise, making the most of every opportunity because the days are evil." Get an upper-hand on Satan by asking yourself these questions: What pressures from the world most affect my spiritual walk? What weakness in my human nature does Satan most often use to undermine my spiritual life? To what direct attacks from Satan am I most susceptible? As you answer each of these questions, bring the answers before God, asking Him to show you how to counteract these deadly forces.

2. How much time are you willing to commit to your relationship with the Lord? To other relationships in your life? Draw a circle and divide it into hours. Chart out how much time you spend in a typical day on the basics of building relationships versus how much you spend on the "stuff" of life—laundry, dishes, bills, work. Look at your circle. Are you happy with what you see? If not, look for specific time-thieves that can be rearranged or deleted in an effort to give you more time for relationships.

3. If your spiritual life is disappointing you, then consider taking a sabbatical from your normal spiritual disciplines for a few days. Use this time to pray, think, and reflect with an open mind on what God is calling you to include as part of your spiritual life. Then, after a week, add one discipline back. Slowly, add back those that seem most fitting to your life and your unique needs.

8

Why Does My Spiritual Life Sometimes Feel Like a Huge To-Do List?

—Kay Arthur

SOON AFTER I WAS SAVED, at the age of twenty-nine, my husband, whom I had divorced three years earlier, committed suicide. At thirty-two, God brought Jack into my life. Jack had been a missionary in Africa and South America for a number of years. Our dates centered around church and conferences, so just before we were married Jack took me to hear Major Ian Thomas, founder and general director of the Torchbearers of the Capenwray Missionary Fellowship in England.

I'll never forget watching Major Thomas as he stood, legs spread to balance himself, excitedly bouncing up and down on tiptoe, proclaiming the profound revelation that seemed to electrify his body. I could almost see the energy flow as he stood, arms outstretched, then pivoting his arms upward at the elbows, his index fingers pointing toward the ceiling. His mouth twitched in excitement as he shared the revelation that had transformed his walk with Christ:

"The Christian life," he almost shouted, "is Christ in you!" With a flip of his wrist, his fingers punctuated his words, then turned from the ceiling toward his body. Then with another unforgettable twist of the wrist, the index fingers twirled around and pointed heavenward again as he said, "And you in Christ!"

With that, an impish smile broke out on his face. "Christianity is not doing. It is being! It is not a life of doing but of simply allowing Jesus to be Jesus in you. . . ."

With his little white mustache moving up and down, almost in rhythm with his bouncing heels, he turned those index fingers from the ceiling to his body again and then straight out toward the audience as he shouted with total conviction, ". . . and Jesus living *His* life through you—Christ is our life! Christ is our life! You're running around doing all these things for God, and you're exhausted. When was the last time God gave someone *your* phone number?"

I sat mesmerized by truth, tears streaming down my face. I was exhausted! I was so busy going to Bible school and attending church every time the doors were open. The church I attended encouraged full participation and a presence at every major event. The school that was affiliated with the church had us record weekly the amount of Bible literature we had distributed and the number of people we had led to Christ. And I was only content with BIG numbers. After all, wasn't all this a sign of my spirituality? But I was exhausted! My "to-do" list was wearing me out.

———— ✑ ————

"When was the last time God gave someone your telephone number?" As I recalled Major Thomas's memorable words, I realized people weren't calling me; I was hotly pursuing them. I felt I must witness to everyone, be at every meeting, constantly doing, doing, doing. After all, wasn't that what God expected of me?

The answer, as I learned that night, was "No!" All my activity might be what others said He expected, but it wasn't bearing witness to my eyes, my heart, and my spirit. I was worn out from trying to live by what I thought my school, my church, and thus, my God expected. I was new to Christianity—eager and full of zeal. I watched others and believed what I was taught. *But I didn't know the truth for myself.*

Set Free

Truth always sets a person free—if it is embraced by the hearer. I was set free the day I listened to Major Thomas. As I went home and thought it all through, I remembered the time Stuart Briscoe came to our school. His message was so radical compared to our usual fare that I was mesmerized then as well. Whether Stuart said it then or later, I cannot remember. I only know that when I think of him, the words he spoke ring in my ears: "God, I can't. You can. Let's go." If your spiritual life seems like nothing but a huge and endless to-do list, let me share some reasons why that happens.

———— ∽ ————

As I said in a previous chapter, we live under grace, not under the Law. Look at your life. Are you living under the Law, thinking, *I must do this, I must do that*? Someone had erroneously taught the Galatians that while they were saved by grace, they were "perfected" by keeping its to-do list—by living under the Law. Someone had bewitched them, and Paul counteracted with his epistle to the Galatians. As Paul asked the churches in Galatia, "Having begun by the Spirit are you now being perfected by the flesh?" (Galatians 3:3, NASB).

Those in Galatia needed to understand that through the Law they died to the Law, that they might live to God. They needed to say as Paul did, "I have been crucified with Christ; and it is no longer I who live, but Christ lives in me; and the life which I now live in the flesh I live by faith in the Son of God, who loved me, and delivered Himself up for me" (Galatians 2:20, NASB).

Becoming a Christian does not make one lawless, rather the Law is fulfilled through the promise of the Spirit as Paul points out in Galatians and in Romans 8:3–4, which reads in part, "For what the Law could not do, weak as it was through the flesh, God did: sending His own Son in the likeness of sinful flesh and as an offering for sin, He condemned sin in the flesh, in order that the requirement of the Law might be fulfilled in us, who do not walk according to the flesh, but according to the Spirit."

The Law can never be fulfilled by living according to a huge "to-do" list. Righteousness can never be attained that way! If it were, none of us would have a chance because we couldn't possibly meet all of the requirements! When we fail to keep one single part of the Law, we have failed to keep all of it.

DON'T MAKE A NOTE OF THAT

I find it hard not to turn my spiritual life into a to-do list because I am a to-do sort of person—a list lady. I love making lists! I have to discipline myself to have a day off from making lists once a week. This helps me be more spontaneous and adaptable! My husband pointed out that I only had fun if I had it on my schedule! It was at that point I decided not to let lists dominate my life.

—Jill

The Law is fulfilled as we walk in the Spirit (Galatians 5:16–26). Remember, spiritual living is possible only through the Spirit, never through the efforts of the flesh.

———————— ❦ ————————

Besides an understanding of what it means to live by the Spirit rather than the Law, in order to rid yourself of your to-do list, the second factor to question is your salvation. Now, don't be alarmed or offended by my suggestion. It's just that I've seen many who thought they were Christians come to know Jesus Christ. These people were not obvious sinners, parading their unrighteousness in the streets, but instead seemingly righteous people sitting in the church pews singing hymns and trying to please God. What they found out was that their righteousness was born of self. They were like the Jews of Jesus' day—people who had a zeal for God but lacked true knowledge. They tried to establish their own righteousness by following the Law, all the time ignorant of the fact that righteousness comes by faith that is born of the Spirit (Romans 10:6–10).

Maybe the reason your spiritual life seems like an impossible to-do list is because it is. You'll never cross off enough on your to-do list to be righteous! And you can't be righteous unless you've been born again—born of the Spirit! When Paul wrote his letter to the Corinthians, he admonished them to examine themselves to see if they were *in* the faith. Remember the basis, the foundation of your spiritual life, is Christ in you. Are you truly His? You can't live by the Spirit if the Spirit isn't in you.

A third factor that can cause your spiritual life to seem like a chore is not knowing or understanding the character of God. God doesn't deal with us according to our performance or according to all we accomplish for Him. Rather He deals with us according to our obedience. The basis of obedience on our part is love, as we are reminded in 1 John 5:3, "For this is the love of God, that we keep His commandments; and His commandments are not burdensome" (NASB). If you will forget your to-do list and simply concentrate on loving the

105

Lord with all your heart, mind, soul, and strength, you'll live a life that is pleasing to Him.

As you spend time in the Old and New Testaments, you'll get to know God, and you'll see that your relationship with God is based on trust, not performance. Performance is really a by-product or the end result of trust. Jesus said our work is to believe. Doing comes from believing.

The fourth and final reason we sometimes find our spiritual life a grind rather than a joy is because we are not living according to what the Word of God says, but instead by the traditions and teachings of man.

When we don't personally know the Word of God for ourselves, when we're not sitting at His feet and listening to Him, all sorts of ideas can be added to our "do-this-if-you-want-to-be-spiritual" list.

Take the case of Mary and Martha in Luke 10:38–42. Martha told the Lord He should be concerned that Mary wasn't helping with the preparations on His behalf. Mary needed to get up off her seat and help Martha! But Martha couldn't move Mary! Mary knew she was right where she needed to be and Jesus confirmed it. Mary had chosen the one thing that was needful while Martha had been distracted by so much that needed doing! Actually the Word shows that Martha's doing for Jesus had drawn her away from Him instead of to Him. "Doing," even on behalf of Jesus, can be very wearing and burdensome when you're not "doing" His bidding. And what is His bidding? You'll never know apart from sitting at His feet!

Are you sitting at the Lord's feet? Are you in the Word of God each day, not for the sake of doing, but for the sake of being? Being in the Word daily allows us to see where we are going. It allows us to discern truth from error. Feeding on the Word is synonymous with living. While the children of Israel wandered the desert for forty years on their way to the Promised Land, God had them gather manna *daily*, because He wanted them to

106

understand that "man does not live by bread alone but by every word which proceeds out of the mouth of God" (Deuteronomy 8:3, NASB).

OVERCOMING WEARINESS WITH WORSHIP

Whenever I don't feel like I want to pray or spend time with God, one thing that helps, even beyond asking the Lord for a hunger and thirst for His Word, is to picture the Lord as my Shepherd. I see myself in His arms as a little lamb. Or I picture the Lord in all the beauty, holiness, and majesty of His throne room. And then I just talk to Him in worship first instead of all my "give-me" prayers. We often get stuck with give-me prayers and miss the aspect of real worship and awe.

—Carole

The Words that Jesus spoke are spirit and life and not burdensome. As you grow in your relationship with Him, as you learn to walk more consistently in the Spirit, as you recognize your impotence and appropriate His all-sufficient grace, you'll forget that silly list you made and instead hear Him say, "Cease striving and know that I am God" (Psalm 46:10, NASB).

Make It Happen

1. To better understand God's grace consider doing an in-depth study of grace. Kay's devotional study book *Lord, I Need Grace to Make It* (Multnomah) is an excellent place to start.

2. Read the book of Galatians and mark every reference to the Law, the flesh, and the Spirit. Next, make a list of what the text of Galatians says about each of these. How is the Law to be part of our life? How are the

Law and the flesh related? What can we expect from living under the control of the Spirit?

3. Pare down your "should" list and the potential for guilt by writing out all the "shoulds" you think are necessary for a growing Christian life. Now compare that list with what Kay has mentioned in this chapter as the essential shoulds and what you have found from reading Scripture. Can you draw a line through any of the shoulds? Can some of the shoulds be turned into valuable, though not essential, spiritual standards?

4. To get a better perspective on the true character of God start a list of "character traits of God." Keep the list in your Bible and each time you come across a character trait in your reading add it to your list and pray that these might be reflected in your life.

9
Can I Really Change?

—Kay Arthur

I WAS DESPERATE. I had sunk into a pit I had dug with my own hands. Try as hard as I might, I couldn't get out. The dreams of my childhood and teen years were shattered. My first marriage ended in divorce, something I never thought would happen to me. The divorce was of my own doing for I could no longer stand living with a manic-depressive.

Now here I was, living like a high-priced harlot, running from the arms of one man to another, looking for unconditional love. I knew my behavior was wrong. I knew that what it was doing to my two precious sons was wrong. I needed to change, to stop—but I couldn't.

What's wrong with me? I cried to God as I became aware of the awfulness of my lifestyle. Suddenly, I became acutely aware of the fact that if I were to stand before God He would justly tell me that I deserved to go to hell. Knowing that, I was determined to change, but nothing happened. I felt like a slave, powerless to help myself, powerless to change. *If I could just begin again,* I thought.

On July 16, 1963, I rolled over in my bed, picked up the phone, and called the physician I worked with at Johns Hopkins Hospital where I was a nurse. "I can't come to work today," I said, "I'm too sick. I'll see you Monday."

I'm sick, I thought, *but there's no cure for my illness because it's not physical.* I crawled out of bed and went downstairs to bake a cake.

In the midst of baking that cake, I felt so overwhelmed that I fled from the kitchen, ran to my bedroom, and fell on my knees beside my bed. "O God, I don't care what you do to me," I pleaded. "I don't care if I never see another man as long as I live. I don't care if you paralyze me from the neck down. I don't care what you do to my two precious sons . . . if you'll just give me peace." Those were the three worst things I could think of that might happen to me! There on my knees I received the Prince of Peace, the Lord Jesus Christ.

In an instant, I was a brand new creature in Christ Jesus. What I couldn't do, God did. I was no longer a slave to sin, for the Son had set me free! On the outside I looked the same, but something had happened on the inside. At that point I couldn't have told you what. I only knew that wherever I went Jesus would go with me.

In the days, weeks, and months that followed all sorts of awesome changes took place. I had a new power within, an ability to say, "No," and stick with it. I didn't know this power was the indwelling Holy Spirit of God. I just saw the changes!

───────── ❧ ─────────

Can you really change as a new creation in Christ? It depends on what you expect to change. Is it your appearance? Your personality? Your abilities? Your character?

If it is your character, then the answer is "yes." As you read the New Testament, Scripture after Scripture testifies to the fact that if you are a true child of God you aren't what you used to be. I'll never forget my delight as a new Christian when I discovered 2 Corinthians 5:17: "Therefore if any man is in Christ, he is a new creature; the old things passed away; behold, new things have come" (NASB). I thought God had put that verse into the Word to describe me. I didn't know then that it applied to every true child of God.

How and why do these changes happen in our character? They happen because your body has become the dwelling place of the Father, Son, and Holy Spirit. As Jesus says in John 14:23, "If anyone loves Me, he will keep my word; and My Father will love him, and We will come to him and make Our abode with him" (NASB). The presence of the Father, Son, and Spirit cannot help but make a difference.

What Changes to Expect

When we look to the Word we gain a better understanding of the type of change God promises will occur when we become new creatures in Christ. Many times we think—and hope—our personality will change, that our natural temperament will suddenly turn into the perfect personality with no flaws. However, personalities are not what God changes. As I said earlier, it is our character that changes. And our character controls our actions rather than changes our personality.

The people of God portrayed in the Word had a variety of personalities and temperaments. God doesn't produce cookie-cutter Christians. He made us each different when He formed us in our mother's womb. God created us as we are for a unique purpose and ordained the days we are to live (Psalm 139:15–16). Sometimes the things we want to change are the very things God chose for us to fill His unique purpose for our lives.

Since being saved in 1963, I have submitted to the Lord the aspects of my character and temperament, like my quick temper, that hinder my Christian walk, but my basic personality has remained the same. And so it should. If we are to be useful servants for God, we cannot abdicate our personalities and try to be like somebody else. Instead, when we become new creatures in Christ, it is primarily our character that must undergo change rather than our personalities.

That's not to say we aren't accountable for those aspects of our nature that tend to make us sin. When we yield our lives to Christ, we submit our whole being—character, personality, and temperament—so that we can grow into a closer likeness of Him.

For instance, as I said, I had an awful temper before I was saved. But now, rarely do I blow up. What keeps me from flying off the handle, even though that would be my natural reaction to maddening situations, is a desire to walk in obedience to Christ. And that reflects a change in my character.

As we begin to understand God's character and as we spend time with Him in His Word and in prayer, our character changes as well. But the changes cut to the core of who we are, beyond our ability to handle anger or rein in a loose tongue. When the Holy Spirit dwells in our heart, we can look for a transformation of our affections, our sensitivity to sin, our abilities, and our desires.

———— ✑ ————

First John 3 and 4 tell us that one of the distinguishing characteristics of a child of God is a heart of love. If we don't love, we are not born from above. Love happens because God, the Supreme Lover, lives inside us. We change because He changes our heart. As Ezekiel and 2 Corinthians teach, under the New Covenant we get a heart of flesh rather than a heart of stone.

This doesn't mean we'll always *feel* a wonderful, overwhelming love for people. The world's definition of love suggests that love is a sentiment or an emotion. God commands us to love, and because you can't command sentiment or emotion, love has to be an action.

First John 5:1–2 further describes the way our heart is transformed: "Whoever believes that Jesus is the Christ is born of God; and whoever loves the Father loves the child born of Him. By this we know that we love the children of God, when we love God and observe His commandments" (NASB). We can witness a change in our affections by the actions we do for others out of love for God.

———————— ∽ ————————

The second major change in character is a new sensitivity to sin. When the Holy Spirit enters us, He convicts us of right and wrong.

Not too long ago, I got mad at Jack. I was trying to explain to him some of my innermost feelings when he picked up the checkbook and asked, "What did you write this check for?"

Here I was pouring my heart out to him and he wasn't even listening! Not only did he interrupt me, but he asked me about something as insignificant as a check! I could feel the fury swelling inside of me and my anger starting to control me.

I gave in. Spurting out a few choice words, I left the room, slammed my Bible down on the bench by the front door, jumped in the car, and drove away. There's no question my actions grieved the Holy Spirit. The whole time I was doing it I knew I was wrong, but I didn't want to do what was right. My flesh was stinging with pain, and I let it have its way.

But does that mean I am no longer saved? No. It simply means I quenched the Holy Spirit. He was there to come to my rescue, but I didn't want rescuing. I could have walked under the control of the Spirit, but I chose sin over righteousness. Because the Holy Spirit was within me, I knew my actions were sin. It wasn't okay to stomp angrily away from Jack, to say mean words about him under my breath as I drove away. While I was driving, the Holy Spirit was saying, "You shouldn't have responded that way."

I remember defending myself, "But Jack should be more sensitive. He should have listened!"

"True, but that's not the issue," the Holy Spirit said to my heart. "You shouldn't have responded as you did." If I weren't saved I'm fairly certain I would have stewed the rest of the day and felt justified in my response. But with the Holy Spirit's prompting, I was convicted of my sin.

———————— ✑ ————————

Along with a new sensitivity to sin comes a new ability to see and hear what the Lord is telling us each day through His Word. No longer are we like the people Jesus refers to in Matthew 13:14, "You will keep on hearing but will not understand, and you will keep on seeing but will not perceive" (NASB).

When God saves us, He opens our eyes. He turns us from darkness to light, the veil comes off our eyes. He leads us and guides us into all truth as the Spirit of God explains to us the things of God, giving us the mind of Christ.

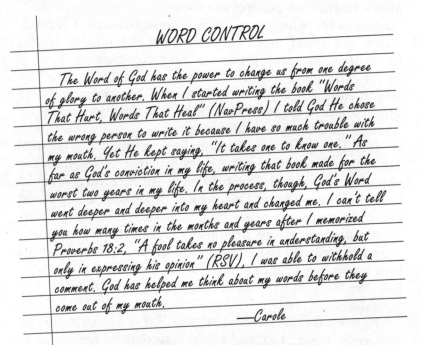

WORD CONTROL

The Word of God has the power to change us from one degree of glory to another. When I started writing the book "Words That Hurt, Words That Heal" (NavPress) I told God He chose the wrong person to write it because I have so much trouble with my mouth. Yet He kept saying, "It takes one to know one." As far as God's conviction in my life, writing that book made for the worst two years in my life. In the process, though, God's Word went deeper and deeper into my heart and changed me. I can't tell you how many times in the months and years after I memorized Proverbs 18:2, "A fool takes no pleasure in understanding, but only in expressing his opinion" (RSV), I was able to withhold a comment. God has helped me think about my words before they come out of my mouth.

—Carole

In Philippians 2:12–13, Paul describes how our yielding to the work of the Spirit within transforms us from without: "So then, my beloved, just as you have always obeyed, not as in my presence only, but now much more in my absence, work out your salvation with fear and trembling; for it is God who is at work in you, both to will and to work for His good pleasure" (NASB).

It's important to clarify the word "work." We are to "work out," or carry out to completion, our salvation. By no means does that imply we work for our salvation. To put it in simple terms, Paul is saying to let God be God in you—don't quench His work. For example, when I was upset with Jack for not listening to me, if I had stopped and allowed God to be God in me, I wouldn't have responded as I did. Although Jack didn't show me the tenderness I would have loved and appreciated, God's grace was adequate, sufficient, and available. I should have obeyed and appropriated what was mine. I should have had the attitude of Jesus—humility—rather than looking out only for my personal interest (Philippians 2:1–11).

———— ✑ ————

Finally, along with our new abilities to understand the Word, God also creates in us new desires, namely a hunger for the things of the Lord. When we ignore that hunger or fill our bellies with the world's chaff, there is a huge void inside that won't go away. How well this is illustrated by stories that have come from behind the Iron Curtain: Christians, young and old, have risked their freedom and often even endangered their lives by going to underground churches and hand-copying the Word of God. There is an appetite for Christ within us that must be satisfied.

Under Construction

While we can expect these four character traits to mature as we grow in the Lord, we must remember that change of any kind is a process. There is no such thing as instant holiness or absolute maturity. The Christian life is one of pressing on. As Paul wrote to the church at Philippi, "Not that I have already obtained it, or have already become perfect, but I press on in order that I may lay hold of that for which also I was laid hold of by Christ Jesus. Brethren, I do not regard myself as having laid hold of it yet; but one thing I do: forgetting what lies behind and reaching forward to what lies ahead, I press on toward the goal for the prize of the upward call of God in Christ Jesus. Let us therefore, as many as are perfect, have this attitude; and if in anything you have a different attitude, God will reveal that also to you" (Philippians 3:12–15, NASB).

Often I see people who try to put their personalities and temperaments under submission to the Lord and expect an overnight transformation. Wouldn't it be wonderful if that happened? But it doesn't happen that way! Many times the big and obvious sins disappear almost immediately, but the transformation into Christlikeness comes at a slower pace.

EATING AN ELEPHANT

We can change, but God is not going to change us without our obedient cooperation. Sometimes it's a little like eating an elephant. We look at the "huge" things that need to be different in our lives and give up before we start. How do you eat an elephant? In bite-size pieces! A bit at a time. Decide which "bit" to start with and given time you'll polish off the whole thing.

—Jill

My book *Lord, Heal My Hurts* (Multnomah) has sold tremendously well because the title appeals to our desire for a quick fix. We want our hurts healed. People want an instant change, so they grab the book with high hopes that after reading a few pages their problems will be solved. Interestingly, I get letter after letter from people who have read the book and say it is the first thing that has brought real healing.

That's because it's a study that takes you deep into the Word of God as you work your way through the book. Answering questions and writing out insights as you study scripture after scripture leads to change and healing. There's such power in the Word of God!

I even remind readers at one point to keep going because often they don't see any hope of change until they're halfway through the book. By the time they finish the book, the change usually takes place, but only after two things happen. First, they have to discover what God's Word has to say regarding their situation, and, second, they have to determine they're going to believe God no matter how they feel or think, and respond accordingly. When they see truth and embrace it, change is inevitable.

Like everyone else, I'm under construction. I wish I were perfect—ideal in every aspect—but I'm not. What I do want to remember, however, is that I can retard or speed up the process to a certain degree by the choices I make. Jesus said, "Blessed are those who hunger and thirst after righteousness for they shall be filled" (Matthew 5:6, NASB). Therefore, I want to do everything I can to keep a strong appetite for the things of God.

Although the changes we long for may not come overnight, we can rest assured that with Christ in us we will change. He who has begun a good work in you will complete it (Philippians 1:6).

Make It Happen

1. Recall what your attitudes were like before you accepted the Lord. What noticeable changes have you seen

in your attitudes and responses when it comes to loving your neighbors, honoring Christ, or being sensitive to sin?

2. Change continues when we choose to renew our minds through hearing and reading the Word. In Romans 12:2, Paul warns us, "Do not conform any longer to the pattern of this world, but be transformed by the renewing of your mind." In other words, don't let the world squeeze you into its mold. Our metamorphosis begins on the inside with the traits of new affections, new desires, new abilities, and a new sensitivity to sin. Eventually, these inner changes become obvious on the outside and the change is complete. Where are you in the process of these changes?

3. If we hope to make our devotion to Jesus pure and simple we must personally read the Word. Consider purchasing a copy of *The International Inductive Study Bible* (Harvest House), and start taking apart each book of the Bible on your own according to the instructions given at the beginning of each book.

4. Write down what you want to change and why. Is what you're hoping to change necessary for God's purpose, or are you instead conforming to man's image? If so, you're going to find yourself living a miserable existence. Learn to trust in God's sovereignty and recognize that some aspects of yourself "the Lord of hosts has planned, and who can frustrate it?" (Isaiah 14:27).

Becoming a Woman of God
Kathy Bence

Who can find a virtuous woman? You know one. But often you see only her faults. "I'm so disorganized." "I'm a hopeless gossip." "I can't seem to conquer criticism." "I need to work on managing my time."

How can I tackle them all at once?

You can't. But you could concentrate on one virtue a week.

Ben Franklin, though not a Christian, worked diligently at increasing virtue in his everyday living. The thirteen virtues he chose to increase were temperance, silence, order, resolution, frugality, industry, sincerity, justice, moderation, cleanliness, tranquility, chastity, and humility.

You may compose a totally different list than Ben's. For lists of virtues, check the Beatitudes (Matthew 5:3–11), the gifts of the Spirit (Romans 12:6–8), the fruits of the Spirit (Galatians 5:22–23), or the virtuous woman passage (Proverbs 31). As you practice a virtue each week, you'll begin to see tangible changes in your life.

1. Choose a virtue for week one.

2. Find relevant Scripture passages and write them on small cards to place over the kitchen sink to memorize.

3. Meditate on the merits of this characteristic. Why is it valuable? How will it enrich me? Why does it please God?

4. During the week, measure your actions by this virtue. For example, if love is your virtue focus, then throughout the week ask: Is this a loving act?

5. Don't set goals or expectations. Simply practice the virtue and try to absorb its meaning.

6. Pray that God will help you understand and absorb each

virtue. Follow His leading in acquiring new (virtuous) habits.

7. Expect some failings and/or hindrances. You cannot conquer a virtue totally in one week.

8. Remember that God is pleased by our intentions as much as our success. Be assured that God will honor your efforts, for all virtue flows from Him. He will aid you in your efforts to grow into His likeness.

—From *Today's Christian Woman* (March/April 1988)

10
Why Do I Sometimes Question My Salvation?

—*Kay Arthur*

THE DAY I ACCEPTED the Lord my life radically changed. My immorality came to a screeching halt! The way I dressed changed as I realized Jesus was now my escort wherever I went. My vocabulary and responses changed. I couldn't get enough of the Word of God.

Those were immediate changes. Then the Lord gently showed me what else had to go. Smoking was the first. When I noticed that none of the Christians I ran around with smoked, I decided I'd quit. It didn't last long. Then one night, while smoking a cigarette as I prayed and read my Bible, I was convicted. As I leaned on the Spirit, I was able to stop.

Not too long after that, while sharing Jesus with a friend over cocktails, the Lord suddenly made me aware that my social drinking was something else I needed to give to Him.

I stood amazed at the changes because I knew they were not of my doing. Then it happened.

I was sitting at a typewriter in my office at Johns Hopkins Hospital when out of the blue I thought, *This stuff about Jesus Christ is a bunch of bull.*

I was horrified! Despite the dramatic changes in my

lifestyle and the healing that had started in my life, the thought came again. *It's just a bunch of bull!* The thought seemed to come from nowhere! As I left work that afternoon, I felt so unclean. That night a group of Christians gathered at my home. In the midst of our sharing, I suddenly burst into tears. Ashamedly I told them of the awful thoughts I'd had that day. Dave, a young man who was discipling me, laughed and said, "Those thoughts aren't yours. That's an attack from the enemy." Much to my relief, he explained that even a Christian can have all sorts of wrong thoughts pop into her head, but it's what she does with them that is important.

--------- ✐ ---------

At one time or another, most of us have been through some sort of experience that causes us to wonder if we really are saved. Those doubts come for varied reasons and in varied ways. And when the doubts persist, we often wonder, "If I'm a Christian, why am I doubting my salvation?" These unexpected and ominous thoughts often catch us off guard. Unless we handle them biblically, they not only leave us shaken, but oftentimes leave us so tormented that we are paralyzed when it comes to serving the Lord. Doubt can stem from three primary sources.

Instigators of Doubt

When it comes to doubts about our salvation, Satan is one of the biggest culprits. He goes for our jugular vein, causing us to question the very foundation of all that we're building our lives on—our salvation. By bombarding us with his fiery darts of doubt, the enemy tries to undermine our effectiveness as witnesses. What right do we have to tell others about salvation if we are uncertain *we're* saved? How can we even pray if we're not certain we're God's children?

In this state of mind, the Word of God, which is meant to be a blessing, suddenly proclaims condemnation on almost every page. Instead of seeing the blessings of those who belong to Him, we become acutely aware of the judgment that will fall on the unrighteous. I have prayed and wept with people who are literally tormented because they can't get any assurance that they are saved. In some instances, the people had good reason to doubt because they weren't saved. However, in other situations this was not the case. Some were tormented by the enemy.

When Satan attacks directly, like he did that day when I was at work, we are not defenseless. No one is immune from these attacks, and it is the epistle of Ephesians that will help us the most in warfare. When I wrote the study devotional *Lord, Is It Warfare? Teach Me to Stand* (Multnomah), I saw that from the very beginning of Paul's epistle he deals with the enemy's tactics head on. He begins with the blessedness of those who belong to God and assures us of God's sovereignty in choosing us in Christ. From then on Paul stresses what it means to be *in* Christ. Paul also warns that we are deceived if we think we are saved and continue to live unrighteous lives.

As Paul brings his epistle to a close, we read those familiar verses in which he tells us how we can defend ourselves against Satan: "Put on the full armor of God, that you may be able to stand firm against the schemes of the devil. . . . Stand firm therefore, having girded your loins with truth, and having put on the breastplate of righteousness, and having shod your feet with the preparation of the gospel of peace; in addition to all, taking up the shield of faith with which you will be able to extinguish all the flaming missiles of the evil one. And take the helmet of salvation, and the sword of the Spirit, which is the word of God" (Ephesians 6:11,14–17, NASB).

Just the fact that part of the armor is the *helmet of*

123

salvation tells us that doubting one's salvation is an area where the Christian will be especially vulnerable. Head wounds are serious! We can expect the enemy to strike at our thought life.

When Satan comes and says, "You're not saved," we can deal with his tactics by checking out each piece of our armor. Our protection comes from believing what God says in His Word, no matter how we feel or think, no matter what others say. Faith extinguishes the enemy's lies. Remember, ours is the shield of faith, and that is why we must be students of the Word—not mere readers. We must know truth for ourselves—firsthand, not secondhand. I cannot stress this enough.

FACTS ARE FACTS

If I'm questioning my salvation, I either don't know God's Word or I'm doubting that God will keep it. John 1:12 says that if I receive Christ, I have been given eternal life. That's the fact. God's very character does not allow Him to lie, so He will do as He has promised (Numbers 23:19). I can know it and believe it.

—Carole

Besides direct attacks from Satan, another source of doubt is sin—the sin of unbelief. Closely related to that is the sin of willful disobedience—stepping over a line drawn by God. When we think of sin we think of adultery, lying, gossiping, or pride. In reality, those are the manifestations of sin.

At the root of all sin is unbelief. What did Adam and Eve do in the Garden of Eden? They listened to the serpent. They believed him rather than God. As a result, they disobeyed God and walked their own way. They chose to act independently of God. Isn't that how Isaiah summarizes it in Isaiah 53:6? Watch for and underline the words *his own way.* "All of us like sheep have gone astray, each of us has turned to his own way; but the LORD has caused the iniquity of us all to fall on Him" (NASB).

For some, the sin of unbelief comes in the form of being unable to believe that God accepts them just as they are—sinners with all the trappings and scars sin brings. Some won't believe that "while we were yet sinners, Christ died for us" (Romans 5:8, NASB). It simply seems impossible that God would love them when they know they are anything but lovable.

Others just found themselves in a state of unbelief regarding various truths, and this unbelief literally prevented them from accepting what God said in regard to their salvation. Others doubt their salvation because they are caught up in a wrong teaching. Let me share a letter I received from a young man I'll call Bill:

> I have always thought Jesus was Savior. I have always had a strong "rock solid" faith in Christ, at least I thought I did.
>
> Last August I came upon a small advertisement in a magazine saying, "Scholarly proof that Flavius Josephus created Jesus. Send $10 to this address." I laughed at the ad. A week later, I was reading a book that had a few references from Josephus that created doubts and unbelief in my head about the historical Jesus and His deity. I began thinking, "What if Josephus did create Jesus?" My thoughts raced back to the magazine ad and all of a sudden my faith in Jesus as my Savior was shattered. I became tired and depressed. I began questioning what the truth really was.
>
> It is as if my beliefs are being manipulated! After I come to the conclusion that one thing is false, like Hinduism or Josephus's alleged creation of Jesus, another weird deluge of doubts and unbelief enter my mind. I am so oppressed with unbelief that I can

hardly muster or maintain an ounce of faith in Christ. I cannot remember being saved before all of this happened. I think I must have opened a channel for Satan to come in and take control of my thoughts, my mind, and manipulate my beliefs.

We each have a choice. Either we believe God, or we believe our feelings, our emotions, and our experiences. We either take Him at His Word, or we live with our evaluation or rationalization of it.

DEEP WITHIN

Shortly after the glow of my dramatic experience of conversion faded I began to doubt my salvation. Because the "feelings" were gone I thought my salvation was gone as well! It's a common tendency to think, "If I don't feel saved, then maybe I'm not." It took me a while to learn that the Holy Spirit comes within to change the very core of our character. He wants to work in our will—in our decision-making processes, whether we feel Him working or not.

—*Jill*

According to Hebrews 3:18–19, unbelief and disobedience go hand in hand. Because we have a choice to either obey or disobey, we can willfully walk contrary to what God says. We sin and sin brings separation. If we are saved, sin doesn't separate us eternally from God, but it does cause a division, a schism in our relationship. Without confessing our sin and seeking reconciliation, a wedge is driven between us and God, and a space for doubt to seep in is opened.

——— ✤ ———

The final source of our doubt comes when we allow

our communication with God to slide—either in our prayer life or in the time we spend in the Word. For instance, I may believe I'm hearing something from God as I pray, but how do I know whether it's God or the flesh? The only way I can tell if what I think I'm hearing is in accordance with God's character and ways is to know what His Word says. God never speaks contrary to His Word.

Sometimes I'm amazed when people share with me what they get out of their prayer time. It's contrary to the Word of God! After asking a few questions, I soon discover they've laid aside the Bible and are merely seeking God through prayer. This approach is extremely subjective and leaves the Christian in a very vulnerable position. The Christian's prayerbook is the Bible. Jesus said, "If you abide in me, and my words abide in you, ask whatever you wish and it shall be done for you" (John 15:7, NASB).

Unique in Every Aspect

In my life, I experienced a very dramatic change when I accepted the Lord. However, not all of us make such dramatic turn-arounds. And for some, this lack of a dramatic testimony can in itself lead to doubts about the authenticity of their salvation. While we do tend to promote the outstanding and dramatic testimony, this certainly isn't the only type of salvation experience. I would love it if mine had been less dramatic, because I would have loved not to have sunk to the depths of sin that I had. Still, when an obvious 180-degree change doesn't happen, we may compare our experiences with others and this comparison can lead to doubt.

How dramatic your salvation experience was often depends upon the environment in which you were raised. If you were raised in the church, grew up with an awareness of the salvation Jesus Christ offers, and kept His commandments, chances are your salvation experience will seem less dramatic than the alcoholic who accepts the Lord and whose life undergoes a radical change overnight. Each person's salvation experience varies. The difference is that those who never lived in fear of the Lord or had a respect for His Law, which guards each of us until we come to faith in Christ, are more likely to have a noticeable outward change.

From what Paul writes about Timothy in 2 Timothy 3, it seems obvious there was never a dramatic outward change of direction in Timothy's life. Timothy knew the Scriptures from childhood and was raised under the influence of a godly mother and grandmother. The Law was his schoolmaster to bring him to Christ. Now take Mary Magdalene's salvation experience. She was a woman cured of evil spirits as told in Luke 8:2. Her change was obvious.

Yet, dramatic or not, both experienced the same thing. Both received the Holy Spirit and moved from the dominion of Satan to the kingdom of God. Both experienced forgiveness of sins. Whether there was blatant manifestation of sin or not, both, like all mankind, were born in sin and, therefore, were sinners. Both walked their own way.

One may have walked more independently of the Law than the other, but both lived in sin. The one who sinned more than the other had a conversion experience that was more obvious, even though both stood in equal need of salvation. It is our changed hearts and the witness of the indwelling Holy Spirit that gives us assurance of our salvation.

What Do You "Know"?

I have studied the book of 1 John and would recommend that anyone who wrestles with doubts about salvation read the book carefully and prayerfully. 1 John was written to help us erase any doubts we may encounter in respect to our salvation. One of John's stated purposes for writing his epistle is found in 5:13: "These things I have written to you who believe in the name of the Son of God, in order that you may know that you have eternal life" (NASB).

Read 1 John in your Bible and circle in colored ink the word *know* each time it appears. After reading each chapter, make a list of what you know and how to know it. Going through 1 John in this manner gives you a tangible way to know if you are truly saved.

For example, 1 John 2:29 reads, "If you *know* that He is righteous, you *know* that everyone also who practices righteousness is born of Him" (NASB). After reading the passage, I know that if I am saved, I will do what is right in God's eyes, not man's.

If you are practicing righteous living, don't let anyone deceive you and say, "You're not a child of God." The one who practices sin as a habit of life is of the devil. The work of the devil is sin. If you are truly born again, God has destroyed that work in your life so that you are no longer under sin's power. You are able to sin (1 John 2:1–2), but you are no longer under sin's dominion that makes sin the habit of your life (1 John 3:5–10).

──────── ⌒ ────────

If you still do not have assurance of your salvation, ask yourself if there is anyone you are not willing to forgive. If so, read Matthew 6:12, 14–15, Mark 11:25–26, and Matthew 18:21–35. Study these passages very carefully. Don't rationalize them. Listen to what Jesus says, take note of how He illustrates His point, and believe Him. A lack of forgiveness may be why you are tormented regarding your salvation. Remember the kingdom of heaven is made up of forgiven people. Although we have sinned greatly against our holy God, we have been totally forgiven—even though we do not deserve it and did nothing to earn God's forgiveness. Forgive and see what happens.

If you still have doubts, do everything you can to resist the enemy. Look at your life and point out the changes I discussed in the previous chapter—new affections, new desires, new abilities, and a new sensitivity to sin—as evidence of your salvation. These changes are the greatest proof of our salvation. Like 2 Corinthians 5:17 says, "Therefore, if any man is in Christ, he is a new creation; the old things passed away; behold, new things have come" (NASB).

If doubts persist, cry out to God. Pour out your heart to Him, for it is His responsibility through His Spirit to bear "witness with our spirit that we are children of God" (Romans 8:16, NASB). Man cannot give you assurance of your salvation, but God can. And if the assurance is not there and you want to be saved and are willing to come to God on His terms, then come. You can know from the Word that even your desire for salvation is from Him. He is calling you, and those who come to Him, He will not cast out. "Everyone who calls on the name of the Lord shall be saved" (Acts 2:21, NASB).

Make It Happen

1. After reading the book of 1 John, what do you see as proof in your life that you are indeed saved? What attitudes and actions in your life are consistent with someone who truly has the Lord Jesus Christ as Lord of her life?

2. If your doubts seem to be out of control, consider making an appointment with your pastor for some counseling. But take action now. Don't let your doubts get a foothold in your life and continue to erode your relationship with Christ. Be up-front with your doubts and don't be concerned that others will think less of you because of your doubts.

3. Look back in your life on those times you have

doubted your salvation. How did you rise above these doubts? What did you learn about yourself and God in the process? What situations lead you to a doubtful heart?

11
What Does It Mean to Be a Joy-Filled Christian?

—Jill Briscoe

I HAVE A MISSIONARY FRIEND who labored for years in France, a difficult mission field because so few there have a real understanding of the gospel or any connection with the church. During her twenty-six years of service, my friend had led very few to the Lord. As her extended furlough to the United States came closer, something happened to every one of those who had made professions of faith. One died. One moved away. The remaining ones fell away from God. For her many years of hard work she was left with nothing to show for her efforts. She wondered what she would tell her home church.

Later my friend wrote me a letter and in it she said, "When I can't praise God for what He has allowed, I praise Him for who He is in what He has allowed." I was so struck by her words that I wrote them in my Bible. My friend, despite the fact that there was little joy in her circumstances, found joy in her God.

———— ✐ ————

In the world's mind, joy is a feeling, a good giggle, a sense of happiness. Stuart, my husband, describes worldly joy like this: "For some people, happiness only happens when their happenings happen to happen the way they happen to want them to happen!" Happiness, in other words, is an emotion that is contingent upon everything going well, or a life with no problems.

Christian joy, however, is different. It has nothing to do with whether our life goes as we want it to. My friend's experience in France perfectly illustrates this truth about Christian joy. I'm certain her heart was breaking as she saw those in whom she had invested her life fall away from the Lord. She could have easily looked back and said, "What a waste. I could have been doing something else."

Instead, she had joy because she knew that in spite of her disappointment, God was at work in her life and she was doing what He wanted her to do. The joy we can expect as Christians is deeper than emotion. After all, the Holy Spirit doesn't come into our hearts to do His deepest work in the shallowest part of us.

———— ✑ ————

If Christian joy isn't a fleeting emotion or a smile, what is it? I've found it helpful to define joy by looking at two of its most vital elements.

First, joy is hope. The opposite of joy is despair. Despair is a dark place where there is no hope of life ever getting any better. Joy whispers, "There *is* hope!" If a despairing person can begin to hope or believe things can change for the better, then joy creeps in. Joy massages the taut neck muscles and relaxes you. Joy and hope are inseparable. We may not "always" experience joy. Sometimes, as the Scriptures say in Psalm 30:5, "Joy comes in the morning" (RSV) after the long, dark night is over. Many times when joy is not felt, it is possible it is there all the time disguising itself as hope—a hope that leads to joy.

Second, joy is confidence. This confidence comes from knowing our God is a God of the future. He is in control of our tomorrows. Knowing He is in charge gives us an overwhelming sense of peace and security. To me, joy is a settled sense of well-being. Joy leads us to trust God. And yet this doesn't just happen to us. We need to cooperate. We need to tell God, "though I am out of control I believe you are in control. Though my life and relationship are disintegrating, I believe you are complete and active though I cannot see you working."

Not long ago, I was praying hard for a terrible situation. The more I prayed, the worse the situation became. *What was God doing?* I fretted. *Why wasn't He busy answering all these earnest petitions?*

We live by the side of a lovely lake and, rising early one morning, I went and sat by it. The surface was like a millpond—still and smooth until a fish jumped up here and there sending ripples across the surface. It was then I seemed to hear the Lord ask me, "Jill, do you have to see the fish jump to believe that it is here?" I wanted to say, "Yes, Lord!" but in reality I knew, and He knew, I *didn't* need to see the fish jump. I knew that underneath that glass-like, still surface the lake was teeming with activity. So I decided to have confidence in the Lord—to trust Him with my heartache and prayers and let Him answer them when He was ready. At that moment, peace came and a measure of joy returned to my unhappy heart.

I believe God, through His Spirit, grants us love, joy, and peace no matter what is happening in our lives. As Christians, we shouldn't expect our joy to always feel like happiness, but instead recognize joy as an inner security—a safeness in our life with Christ.

As joy-filled Christians should we always wear a perpetual smile on our faces? No. As I've just said, at times life is tough and we don't feel cheerful. I've told women going through hard times, "You're not going to feel very good. I don't expect you to smile." The relief I see on the faces of women who are told they don't have to wear an artificial smile is amazing. Like these women I counsel, we, too, can take comfort in knowing we can be somber, serious, even burdened, yet still have joy.

How Joy Happens

Our joy as Christians is not based on circumstances, but rather on being in God's will and doing what we were created to do. If we are living as God wants us to live, we will feel a sense of inner peace, and that is the joy we are promised as Christians.

Where some of us stumble, however, is in thinking joy from being in God's will should equal feelings of happiness. That isn't always the case, as my missionary friend articulated so well in her letter. Doing God's will doesn't guarantee you'll *feel* happy about the position you're in. In fact, you might very well be unhappy in certain situations where God calls you to serve.

MAKING THE RIGHT CHOICE

My greatest times of joy come when I consciously make the choice to believe God and to do what He says no matter the pain, no matter the difficulty of the situation, no matter the humbling process. When I tell my Father this is what I'll do, there is such a sweet sense of joy because I know I've made the right choice, and that pleases Him.

—Kay

During one point in our ministry, Stuart was on the road for long periods of time. There was absolutely no question in either of our minds that we were in the center of God's will. But I can tell you there were many lonely hours and days, even months, when God's will didn't feel like too much fun at all! And yet, I knew if

Stuart stayed home, I'd feel a whole lot worse than if he was away! "How is that?" you may ask. Because you can't experience lasting joy if you deliberately turn away from God and what He has given you to do. To be holy rather than happy then becomes your choice. And the choice to be holy brings joy.

The pursuit of holiness won't always be a happy venture. If you doubt that, just read any of the Gospel accounts of Christ's death. Hebrews 12:2 reads, "Let us fix our eyes on Jesus, the author and perfecter of our faith, who for the joy set before him endured the Cross, scorning its shame, and sat down at the right hand of the throne of God." Jesus didn't enjoy the Cross. Instead, He endured the Cross for the joy that would follow.

Time for Soul-Searching

A woman at our church came to me for guidance when she noticed a sense of joy absent from her life. She desperately wanted her sense of joy to return.

"Let's find out where you lost your sense of joy," I said.

"No, no," she said. "I don't want to do that. I just want it back."

But I persisted and said, "You can't get it back until you figure out why you lost it."

This young woman hedged for nearly an hour, trying to avoid this essential question. Finally she admitted the day her joy disappeared was the day she moved in with her boyfriend. Facing this fact was difficult for her. She wanted her joy back without confession, action, or obedience. Christian joy, she discovered, has conditions. If she wanted joy to return, she first needed to be in obedience to God's Word, and, clearly, living with a boyfriend goes against God's commands. Second, she needed to confess her sinful behavior. And finally, she had to take action—she had to move out of her boyfriend's apartment.

————— ↝ —————

If joy has left your life, it's time to do some soul-searching. Begin by making certain you truly understand what Christian joy is. Joy isn't a feeling, but instead a sense of peace and confidence in God. If your understanding of true joy is on target, then ask yourself, "Where did I lose my joy and why? What has changed in my life?"

This young woman knew something was wrong because she lacked peace. Look for those outward signs that something is off in your relationship with Christ. Remember, too, circumstances can't rob us of our joy if those circumstances are within the will of God.

The young woman who lived with her boyfriend lost her sense of joy because she put herself in circumstances that were displeasing to God. She discovered, too, that the pleasures of sin brought her only superficial happiness. The devil didn't warn her that her happiness would be short-lived.

Often couples living in sin tell me, "But we're happy. How could we be happy if we weren't doing what God wants?" My response is, "Come back next year and tell me if you're still happy. Without a doubt, there will come a time in your life where your happiness runs out on you because your happiness depends on your happenings. Where will you be when your lover runs off with someone else?"

Joy comes from being centered on the eternal constant—God. It also comes from living in obedience to Him. It won't come when it is dependent on the fickleness of human nature, material possessions, our surroundings, or even our relationships.

When I look at some women's lives I'd be the first to admit they have little reason for joy. These women are in tough situations—living with a verbally abusive spouse, or worse. They might be struggling with a wayward child or caring for a sick parent. But we can all have joy despite the circumstances when we do what my missionary friend did—she kept her heart fixed on God.

FINDING TRUE JOY

The older you get the more you realize there is not a lot of joy in life. If it's not in your heart, you're not going to have joy. Sure, it's great to have a husband who loves you, or a wonderful child. But those things are only a small imitation of the joy that we can get from the reality of knowing God.

—Carole

Hannah of the Old Testament is a beautiful example of a woman who found joy despite tough times and difficult choices. Hannah was barren, and her husband's second wife, Peninnah, provoked Hannah to the point of tears about her lack of children. Hannah prayed for a child and promised she would give the child to the Lord if her prayer was answered.

Hannah kept her promise and presented her four-year-old son, Samuel, to be raised by the wicked men at the temple. Then Hannah returned to the conflict in her home and a woman who hated her. Yet, after handing over Samuel and returning home to an unchanged situation, she was able to say, "My heart rejoices in the LORD; in the LORD my horn is lifted high" (1 Samuel 2:1). Her heart was filled with joy.

Hannah was able to sing this psalm with the empowerment of God. Her focus wasn't on her problems, but instead on the Lord, and joy was hers.

Make It Happen

1. Look up the following passages: Psalm 4, 2 Corinthians 1:3–5, 1 Peter 4:13, and Romans 15:13. As you meditate on these passages, how is joy described? If you

were asked for a single sentence definition of joy, what would it be?

2. To get a better understanding of what Christian joy involves, consider reading the writings of Corrie ten Boom, Joni Eareckson Tada, or Stormie Omartian. Each of these women have triumphed over circumstances to find joy in their lives.

3. Where is your joy centered? Is it in human relationships, your career, your possessions? If joy seems to elude you, then make changes to move the focus from your circumstances to God. Study the Scriptures. Ask questions of those you admire who seem to lead a joy-filled life. Bring before God your request for a life centered on Him.

Making the Tough Times Count
Joni Eareckson Tada

God wishes to instill within each of us a strong desire for the imperishable, the incorruptible, the inheritance that never perishes, spoils, or fades. But in order to grip our hearts with those promises, God sometimes takes drastic measures. You and I don't appreciate His method of operating at first, but later we're grateful for it.

That's exactly what God did for me when he sent a broken neck my way. He blew out the lamps in my life that lit up my here and now so captivatingly. The dark despair of my paralysis wasn't much fun. But it sure made those resurrection promises come alive.

And that brings up one of God's primary objectives: *Suffering gets us ready for the resurrection.*

How do pain and problems get us ready? Broken necks, broken homes, and broken hearts crush our hopes that earthly things can satisfy. Only the promise of the resurrection can truly move our eyes from this world. The glorious day when "we will be whole" becomes our passion as we realize, once and for all, that earth can never meet our deepest longings.

Suffering prepares us to meet God when we get there.

Just think. Suppose you never knew pain. No stained reputation. No bruised feelings. No sore back, twisted ankle, or decayed molars. How could you appreciate the scarred hands with which Christ will greet you? What if no one had ever offended you deeply? How could you adequately express your gratitude when you approach the Man of Sorrows who was acquainted with grief?

When you meet Jesus face to face, your headaches and

141

hardships will have given you a taste of what He went through to purchase the promise of your resurrection. And your loyalty to Him in your own suffering will give you something concrete to offer Him in return. For what other proof could you bring of your love and faithfulness if this life left you totally unscarred?

If in our trials we are faithful, *suffering wins us rich rewards in heaven.* It's not so much that the resurrection will be wonderful in spite of all our pain—it will be wonderful *because* of it. My wheelchair, unpleasant as it may be, is what God uses to dislocate my stubborn resentment and dislodge my self-centered attitudes. My wheelchair even forces me to be more faithful to Him. The more faithful I am to Him, the more rewards are stored up in heaven. Earthly sufferings don't simply aid us today, they will serve us in eternity.

—From *Today's Christian Woman* (March/April 1991)

12
Who Does God Bless and How?

—Kay Arthur

WHAT WOULD YOU SAY if someone asked you, "What evidence do you have that God has blessed you?" Would you take an inventory of your success, your bank account, your health, the size of your home, or the state of your relationships? Don't be surprised if that's your natural inclination.

By the world's standards, and unfortunately the standards of some Christians, wealth, good health, success in business, and the world's recognition are obvious signs of a life that is blessed. However, the world's standards are a far cry from the biblical interpretation of blessings.

What does it mean to be blessed by God? I have found no better place to look for the answer than in Matthew 5–7. Jesus' incredible Sermon on the Mount came as He withdrew with His disciples and began to teach them, saying,

> Blessed are the poor in spirit, for theirs is the kingdom of heaven. Blessed are those who mourn, for they shall be comforted. Blessed are the gentle, for they shall inherit the earth. Blessed are those who hunger and thirst for righteousness, for they shall be satisfied. Blessed are the merciful, for they shall receive mercy. Blessed are the pure in heart, for they shall see God. Blessed are the peacemakers,

for they shall be called sons of God. Blessed are those who have been persecuted for the sake of righteousness, for theirs is the kingdom of heaven. Blessed are you when men cast insults at you, and persecute you, and say all kinds of evil against you falsely, on account of me. Rejoice, and be glad, for your reward in heaven is great, for so they persecuted the prophets who were before you. (Matthew 5:2–12, NASB)

The reasons for blessing and the ensuing teaching that followed amazed the multitudes who joined Jesus and the disciples on that mountainside overlooking the Sea of Galilee. His words and His authority were disconcerting. This teaching was so contrary to what they had heard from the religious teachers of their day! These were the blessed? The poor in spirit, those who mourned, the meek, the persecuted? The world deemed these as losers—not winners!

And how were they blessed? With blessings that had nothing to do with material prosperity! These blessings seemed intangible—at least for the present time. They were more of a spiritual nature, blessings that would minister more to the inward soul of man rather than to the creature comforts of life.

What were these blessings? Think through what Jesus said in the Beatitudes. The blessings include the kingdom of heaven, comfort, inheriting the earth, satisfaction, receiving mercy, seeing God, being called the sons of God, and a reward in heaven. And who would receive these blessings? The poor in spirit, those who mourned, the gentle, the ones who hungered and thirsted for righteousness, the merciful, the pure in heart, the peacemakers, those who were persecuted, insulted, and falsely accused. And these blessings would be theirs solely because of their identification with Jesus Christ!

No wonder the multitudes were amazed. How contrary all of this was not only to what the world thought, but to what many of the religious leaders of the day thought, taught, and pursued.

———— ✐ ————

Take, for example, how the poor in spirit are blessed. What does it mean to be poor in spirit? The parable of the Pharisee and the tax collector in Luke 18:9–14 sheds some light on this question. This parable speaks of two men who went up to the temple to pray—one a Pharisee and the other a tax collector. "The Pharisee stood and was praying thus to himself, 'God, I thank Thee that I am not like other people; swindlers, unjust, adulterers, or even like this tax-gatherer. I fast twice a week; I pay tithes of all that I get.' But the tax-gatherer, standing some distance away, was even unwilling to lift up his eyes to heaven, but was beating his breast, saying, 'God, be merciful to me, the sinner!' " (NASB).

Jesus' words are memorable in verse 14, "I tell you this man went down to his house justified rather than the other; for everyone who exalts himself shall be humbled, but he who humbles himself shall be exalted" (NASB).

The good self-image the Pharisee had of himself kept him from seeing his abject poverty before God. The word for poor, used in this beatitude, is an interesting one. It doesn't mean that a person is lacking some of the basics of life. It means that one is so destitute he can't even raise his head! Those who come to God and are able to offer Him absolutely nothing are blessed! Why? Because they know it is only due to God's grace—grace through faith—that they can even come before Him. It is through no merit of their own, not through any good works they might do. Their presence is allowed based on pure, unmerited favor.

And what do those who approach the Lord with this knowledge receive? What is their blessing? The kingdom of heaven and all that goes with it—including adoption into the family of Christ, the King of Kings.

Do you look around at others and compare your life and your material prosperity to others? Do you sometimes wish you could be more than what you are or have more than what you have?

Why? If you have the kingdom of heaven and can call the King, "Abba, Father," what more do you need? Aren't you blessed among mankind? What manner of love the Father has bestowed upon you that you should be called a son of God! Thank Him for so great a love! Ask Him to forgive you for your murmurings, your jealousies, your futile, wishful thinking that has preoccupied your mind.

BOUNTIFUL BLESSINGS

God blesses all who come to Him. He blesses us with forgiveness for our sin. He blesses us with knowledge of himself. He blesses us with means for living a spiritual life—with fellowship, with His Word. Sometimes He blesses us with enough pain to make us more sensitive to others, or enough ill-health or trouble to drive us to himself. These, too, are God's blessings.

—Jill

When you first study the Beatitudes they may not seem like a path to understanding God's blessings. However, the truths in this portion of Scripture take on new meaning when you ask yourself, "How does this state that leads to blessing bring me to a deeper relationship with the Lord?"

For instance, take the second beatitude, "Blessed are those who mourn, for they shall be comforted" (Matthew 5:4, NASB). Think back to times of tears and grief in your life. In the midst of times of testings and trials, many don't recognize these as times of blessings. But they are if you understand what Jesus means when he says, "Blessed are those who mourn for they will be comforted." If we never mourned, if we never shed a tear, we would never be able to experience the blessing of comfort that can come from the Lord.

Time and time again, I've heard people say, "Yes, what I went through was painful and heartbreaking, *but* I wouldn't change for anything what I experienced with the Lord as a result of it." I've heard numerous stories from our Precept students who tell me they are richer for having experienced horrendous trials because they know in greater depth the truth of the fact that God is sovereign and that He has a purpose in trials. Because they responded to trials with faith instead of reacting in bitterness, they have come to know their God in a more intimate way and have been strengthened in the very process. They have come to know what it means to be held close to the breast and feel the heartbeat of their El Shaddai—their all-sufficient God.

My heart grieves at so much of what I see propagated over television in the name of Christianity. It makes me more determined to teach people to study God's Word for themselves so they can distinguish truth from error. How often do you hear, "God is so good! I've been blessed with health, wealth, and happiness!" Is God only good if we receive these kinds of blessings? When you hear this kind of teaching and testimony you can begin to think that material possessions or health are what blessing should look like—if you don't know the Word.

Frankly, when people buy into this kind of blessing mentality, they fail either to understand or to claim the true promises of God that do not assure us exemption from trials and difficulties, but rather His preservation in the midst of them. Often they become disillusioned and even embittered with God because He didn't come through for them the same way that He did for others.

When I watch these programs I think, "I'd like to take you to Romania or Russia and let you talk to the believers there." Precept Ministries has an international outreach, and we worked in both countries before the fall of communism. Sometimes I wonder if the believers there aren't far more blessed of God than Americans. It seems their intimacy with God and with their families—intimacy born out of circumstances: poverty, mourning, and suffering—is well worth the price they've paid. After visiting with the people, being in their homes, and hearing their stories, I thought, "We don't know what rich is!"

Material abundance can often be a distraction rather than a blessing. These people have riches we'll never experience apart from God's purifying fire! The proof of their faith in enduring the fire is more precious than gold.

Blessing in Disguise

Blessings are often not seen because they are delayed—disguised for a while in the form of trials. A son or a daughter who is breaking your heart now may become God's brand, plucked from the fire, set aglow for Him, and used mightily in the advancement of His kingdom.

This morning in my quiet time I was reading Luke 1 and I thought about Elizabeth. It was a heartbreak and a disgrace among men for a Jewish woman not to have children. While all the other young women her age were conceiving children, Elizabeth remained barren month after month, year after year. When she and her husband, Zacharias, were well advanced in age, God took away her disgrace.

Elizabeth would have the privilege of giving birth to John the Baptist, the forerunner of her Savior. How awesome the end of her story is! God had that blessing in mind for her before the creation of the world. Elizabeth just didn't realize it.

UNEXPECTED BLESSING

After Jack left his first job as an associate pastor, we moved to Long Beach, California, to run a center for U.S. servicemen. On top of the work of scrubbing floors, making beds, and preparing meals for these men, I had to take care of our preschool-age daughter. I could have easily viewed this situation as a prison. But now I see that God took this time in my life and turned it into a glorious opportunity to teach me deep lessons in my heart about what it meant to serve Him.

—Carole

Even Paul makes reference to how we need to put the problems we face daily into perspective. In 2 Corinthians, Paul calls our daily trials "light afflictions." And that's what they are—light afflictions, no matter how heavy—if you weigh them in the balances of eternity. In the midst of the hardships we all face, in one form or another, Paul reminds us to look beyond such afflictions when he says, "Therefore we do not lose heart, but though our outer man is decaying, yet our inner man is being renewed day by day. For our momentary, light affliction is producing for us an eternal weight of glory far beyond all comparison, while we look not at the things which are seen, but at the things which are not seen; for the things which are seen are temporal, but the things which are not seen are eternal" (2 Corinthians 4:16–18).

A life that is blessed by God does not mean a perfect life, a problem-free existence. Admittedly, at some point we all pursue the perfect life largely because we're influenced by a world that promises such an existence is just around the corner. Until I was saved, I was in search of it. I was sure the idealistic world I saw portrayed in the movies while I was growing up really existed. Now, I realize that blessedness is being and doing what God wants me to be and do. And although we may encounter many trials along the way, we can count it all joy as James 1 teaches.

Our trials will be as diverse as the shapes and colors we see in a kaleidoscope. But it is through these very trials that our faith works patience—and that in itself is a blessing, for it brings us to greater Christlikeness.

Who Are the Blessed?

We've all seen it before on television. The sports team wins the title and the cheering fans chant, "We're number one, WE'RE NUMBER ONE." The chant gets louder and the index fingers go up as the faces of the fans crowd closer into the camera. Is being "number one" or a perfect "10" a sign of God's blessing? Are these the winners—the ones who will take the prize? Not according to God. It's the meek, the gentle who inherit the earth.

Look at the world's celebrities, the heroes of today. The ones we are so eager to know all about, to imitate, to be with. Do you see them hungering and thirsting after righteousness, or do they parade their sin without blushing? Do they seem satisfied? Fulfilled? Or do they always seem to be searching for something different, something new? Wanting more, more, more—of something, of anything! Are they blessed?

Is it the merciful in this world who make it, or is it those who step on others to get what they want—to reach the top? Won't they someday need mercy? Will they receive it? Are they blessed?

Immorality abounds. It's flaunted and encouraged while purity is put down. Are the impure blessed? In the eyes of the world, it seems so for now. They seem to have the fun—the girls, the guys, the dates, the affairs, the passionate encounters, the thrills, and the naughty or daring experiences. But unless they repent they will never see God. How incredibly sad.

And what about those who aren't going to take anything from anyone? Those who unload their minds, spill their guts, belch their anger, vomit their wrath, and then walk away feeling better for having gotten it off their chest. They really let them know where they stood! Does such "courage," such "dumping" bring blessing?

Are the bitter and unforgiving blessed? Look at their faces. Watch their body language. Do they look like sons of God?

God's blessings are so different from the world's, aren't they? And the blessed—are they easier to recognize now?

Are you among them?

Make It Happen

1. To have a fuller understanding of God's blessings, consider completing Kay's Bible study *Sermon on the Mount*. This study is an in-depth look at the Beatitudes.

2. Match your life up to God's definition of blessing. Do you recall the last time you mourned over a sin yet found comfort and forgiveness from the Lord? Or when was the last time you showed mercy to another, only to later experience the wonderful blessing of God's mercy for you? Blessings are those things that drive us closer to God. What in your life is doing that—making you more and more dependent upon Him?

3. Read Matthew, chapters five through seven in their entirety. What do these chapters say to you about blessings? Would it be possible to uphold any of the standards set forth in these chapters without Christ?

4. Read 1 Peter and mark every occurrence of the

words *suffering* and *glory*. List what you see from marking those words. Look at the blessings in your life. After reading and underlining those key words, what do you hope your blessings will include?

13

Why Is Forgiveness So Difficult?

—*Carole Mayhall*

FORGIVENESS IS WITHOUT A DOUBT a monumental act. Even though we each face it throughout life, forgiveness is complex and unnatural. Each of us has a different understanding of what it involves. To one woman it means forgiving a mother who never loved her; to another, the person who sexually assaulted her. And to yet another it means forgiving a friend who gossiped and betrayed a confidence.

A short time ago I was with a small group of women who shared several deep and terrible hurts in their lives. As I listened, I thought, *I've never experienced any of these tremendous problems. How can I ever hope to help these women in pain?*

Downhearted about what I'd heard that day, I made it a point that night to spend extra time with the Lord. As I poured out my concerns, I felt Him speak to my heart.

"Carole," He said, "the problems may be terribly complex and different in every case, and you may not have the answers, but I do. And I've written them out for you in my Word." God led me to Psalm 19:7–11 and, as I read it, I was amazed and awed by God's answers.

Though the problems of my friends were unbelievably complex, each person had some basic need—a need for joy in the midst of pain, or wisdom as to what to do.

153

Psalm 19 reads, "The law of the LORD is perfect, reviving the soul. The statutes of the LORD are trustworthy, making wise the simple. The precepts of the LORD are right, giving joy to the heart. The commands of the LORD are radiant, giving light to the eyes."

When I'm despairing, I need reviving in my soul. When I'm wondering what to do, I need wisdom. When I'm discouraged and despondent, I need joy. When I'm totally confused, I need light. Exactly!

Today we have support groups that help us identify the root of our problems and offer comfort, but often they don't offer *the* answer that will allow us to move beyond our pain. They don't lead us to the truth—the truth that comes in Jesus Christ and the freedom that comes from knowing and obeying His Word. While we can identify our hurts and pains, all other avenues, except Christ, cannot enable us to forgive and move on.

As Christians we know that because Jesus has forgiven us, we should—we are commanded to—forgive others as Ephesians 4:32 says, "Be kind and compassionate to one another, forgiving each other, just as in Christ God forgave you."

We know that no matter how horrible the situation, God's Word—His precepts—can bring us joy and move us beyond the pain we feel. But knowing it and doing it are two different matters, aren't they? Sometimes we have buried the problem so deep we aren't even aware of it. Sometimes we are so angry, we don't want to obey God and forgive. Sometimes, even though we want to, we just don't seem to be able to forgive.

No one said forgiveness was easy. And it certainly isn't automatic.

Forgiving Past Hurts

A number of years ago, while Jack and I were attending a conference in another state, an acquaintance of mine insisted that we sit down and talk. I agreed, only to discover that her motive behind our get-together was to share three things she didn't like about me.

The first fault she cited was based on a time she tried to tell me a problem and I didn't listen to her entire story. Now, I know I'm a talker, and at times I don't wait until a person finishes before I'm offering advice and answers. Knowing this, it wasn't difficult for me to say, "I'm really sorry. Will you forgive me?"

No sooner had I offered my apology than she cited the second fault. She didn't like my laugh. As she continued, I realized the attack was getting personal. She accused me of laughing loudly in an effort to draw attention to myself. As she touched my arm to make her point, I could feel my resentment rising. I swallowed hard after she detailed this second fault and I mumbled, "Sorry."

The third fault she described was a personal attack that had no basis in truth. It was so sick and offensive that I have promised myself never to foul another person's mind with what she said. After she finished, I walked away stunned.

I cried for two days after this incident. Whenever I tried to tell Jack what had happened, I would break down in tears. When I finally told him the story he said, "Honey, forget it." Jack knew this woman was projecting her own bitterness about life onto me. Even though I believed this was the case too, I couldn't forget her hurtful words. They hung over me like a black cloud. Yet despite my hurt, I knew I had to forgive her. Because of the nature of this woman's attack and the fact that she lived far away from Colorado, I knew forgiveness would have to be one-sided. This was one situation where I didn't feel the Lord leading me back to this woman with hopes of talking things out.

"Lord," I said, once we were back home, "you said to forgive, so I forgive this woman." I handed it over to the Lord, but, to my surprise, my bad feelings about her popped right back. The next day, I repeated my prayer.

"Lord, I forgive this woman. I really mean it. I want to forgive her. Here it is." Again, the whole situation resurfaced.

When we don't forgive, a sense of bitterness grows and the fallout affects more than just the relationship where forgiveness is needed. This woman's hurtful words had encroached on my entire life to the point where Hebrews 12:15 was literally coming true—"See to it that no one misses the grace of God and that no bitter root grows up to cause trouble and defile many."

First, my relationship with God began to suffer. Rather than meditating on what was right and true and pleasing to the Lord, I would rehearse that awful conversation I'd had with that woman, all the time thinking of what I should have said to her attacks.

Our marriage was the next relationship to suffer from my growing sense of being wrongfully accused. Jack deserves to live with a lighthearted wife. That doesn't mean I shouldn't share my burdens with him, but he shouldn't have to deal with what we call in our house a DRA—Dirty Rotten Attitude. Though I may have burdens, I also have a burden bearer and I needed to release those troubles to Jesus rather than dump them on Jack.

Besides these two relationships, my friendships suffered too. *What are they thinking about me?* I sometimes wondered. *Were they secretly thinking horrible thoughts about me? Will they, too, let me have it when I least expect it?*

By not fully forgiving this woman for the hurt she caused me, I allowed her words to become like a pebble thrown into a pond. The ripples it caused grew bigger and bigger until the whole pond was affected.

TURN TO PRAYER

If I struggle with forgiveness it is usually for one of two reasons. First, I have not taken time to understand the reason behind why the person who hurt me acted as he did, and second, I haven't meditated on the "size" of God's forgiveness where I'm concerned. The temptation is to "feed" our wounds and keep them open and bleeding. Prayer is a grand place to start the healing process and find answers to our struggles. It is in prayer we can let our resentment and bitterness go.

—Jill

I handle the vast majority of life's difficulties on a moment-by-moment basis: Something happens, I take it to God in prayer, He gives me wisdom and grace to handle it. But every once in a while, I am faced with a problem of a different sort that isn't handled so easily—unreasonable fear, despair that takes me captive, or, in this case, bitterness that I can't seem to relinquish.

In these situations, Isaiah 40:31 has been the key for me: "Those who wait for the LORD will gain new strength; they will mount up with wings like eagles, they will run and not get tired, they will walk and not become weary" (NASB).

This type of waiting described in Isaiah is of a special kind. I "wait for the Lord" when I spend time daily with Him, but for those situations that don't seem to be taken care of each day, a further step is needed and it is the kind of waiting that *means business.*

Confession is required before we can undertake this kind of waiting. We must ask God if there is anything in our lives that is preventing us from obtaining His grace to forgive. I pray in the light of Psalm 139:23–24,

"Search me, O God, and know my heart; test me and know my anxious thoughts. See if there is any offensive way in me, and lead me in the way everlasting."

I come with paper and pencil to write down—and then confess—those things God brings to my mind. Many times, when I search my heart, God reveals to me something I never thought of—a little dark corner of my life I have refused to disclose to Him. Yet, in this particular case, I had done that. I had confessed everything I knew to confess.

Jack and I were scheduled to return to the town where the incident had occurred and I was getting desperate! I knew I would see this woman, and I knew I hadn't truly forgiven her. So shortly before we were to leave, I went into my study, shut the door firmly, got down on my knees and said, "Lord, I don't know what is causing me not to be able to forgive this person, and I feel so helpless. But you have promised me grace for everything I need. Right now I need help to release this situation; to forgive; to experience your peace. I am not going to leave this place until you supply what I need."

I call this my "wrestling with God" experience. Remember Jacob in Genesis 32 who wrestled with the angel all night and refused to let go until he received a blessing? Well, I felt like I could not let this issue go until I felt the Lord's healing and affirming presence.

As I waited and prayed, I didn't feel a tremendous sense of relief—like I was handed a huge sack of His grace as I sometimes do. Rather, this time, I heard the still, small voice of His Spirit saying, "Carole, I have taken care of it." The black cloud that had hung over me for so long disappeared. The ability to forgive came when I was willing to *wait* an extended time with the Lord.

It seems to me that there are times in most of our lives when the battles are most fierce, when the enemy comes in like a flood, when we need what I call a 100-pound sack of God's grace for the trials we are experiencing. When we are overwhelmed, inundated, feeling helpless and hopeless, left without recourse or strength, it is then we have a unique opportunity to see and know God in His greatness. We find He really is the Victor. We understand He truly can meet all our needs; fulfill all His promises; and do *exactly* what He said He would.

I realized my own helplessness and dependency during that time of being gripped by bitterness. The blackness of my own heart was revealed again to me—the awfulness of an imprisoned soul. This time of waiting also revealed to me a God who is there, one who isn't satisfied with my halfhearted obedience, one who keeps His promises—a God who is *real*.

The following day, Jack and I were back in the section of the country where this entire lesson in forgiveness started. We walked into a crowded room and I spied one empty chair in the front—next to the woman who had caused me so much pain. I sat down beside her and knew for certain I had forgiven her. No longer did I seek revenge or harbor feelings of animosity and hatred.

Moving Past Hurt

The events in our lives that require forgiveness are fraught with hurt and pain, even after forgiveness is given. On occasion, I still had fiery darts from Satan hit me as I thought about my experience with that woman. But they were easily handled by recognizing these digressions as Satan's ploy to undermine my ability to forgive and by turning any negative feelings back to the Lord.

"Forgiveness is hard—especially in a [relationship] tense with past trouble, tormented by fears of rejection and humiliation and torn by suspicion and distrust," says David Augsburger in *Cherishable: Love and Marriage* (Herald Press). He goes on to say: "Forgiveness hurts. Especially when it must be extended to a [person] who doesn't deserve it, who hasn't earned it, who may misuse it. It hurts to forgive.

"Forgiveness costs. Especially in a [relationship] when it means accepting instead of demanding repayment for the wrong done, when it means releasing the other instead of exacting revenge, when it means reaching out in love instead of relishing resentment. It costs to forgive."

LEAVE IT TO GOD

Forgiveness is difficult because we don't want to let the offender off the hook. We want to be the judge, but only God can fill that role. God will justly judge. We are commanded to forgive, and if we don't, bitterness will creep in and destroy us and others (Hebrews 12:15).

—Kay

When I am unable to forgive or move past the pain that remains after forgiveness is granted, this can eat at me like an acid. And, ultimately, the person who pays the biggest price in the relationship is *me*.

I learned about the cost of forgiveness when a close, long-time friend turned from being loyal and supportive to accusing and judgmental of me. In one afternoon she leveled me with harsh words. My heart was broken by her remarks. While I was readily able to forgive her, I didn't know how to handle the relationship in the days that followed. The hurt remained although I'd forgiven her.

Do I avoid her? Do I shut her out of my life? Do I pretend nothing has happened? I struggled with what to do next. Then one day I was reading in Matthew 26, which describes the events that took place in the Garden of Gethsemane. The Lord seemed to grab both my shoulders to get my attention.

While in Gethsemane, Jesus opened His heart to His closest friends—Peter, James, and John. "My soul is overwhelmed with sorrow to the point of death. Stay here and keep watch with me"(Matthew 26:38), He asked of them. Instead, they fell asleep. When He returned to His disciples, He asked for their support again, but they failed Him and fell asleep.

The third time He found them asleep He didn't even wake them! It was as though He thought, *I realize you're going to need your sleep. I love you so much, I'll just let you sleep.*

Later, when Judas betrayed our Lord, Jesus replied, "Friend, what do you come for?" Jesus referred to Judas as friend, even though he knew Judas's betrayal would lead him to the terrible pain of the Cross. If you or I had met Judas, we'd probably say, "You horrible betrayer, Judas Iscariot." Yet the first word out of Christ's mouth was "Friend."

If Christ was to be my example, then I knew I needed to continue to show love to my friend no matter how she acted or responded. I did just that—even though it hurt. I tried many times to go back to her and talk things through, but she refused. She felt she was right in what she said about me and I had to accept that. The intensity of our friendship changed—no longer did we share our hearts. The loss of our relationship as I once knew it felt like a death in my life, but my heart remained at peace because not only was forgiveness present, but I knew I was doing what God commanded.

———— ∽ ————

It's a fallacy to think human relationships won't have hurts. The first three words of M. Scott Peck's book *The Road Less Traveled* (Touchstone) are "Life is difficult." Even Scripture bears this out with the words of Paul in 2 Corinthians 6:10, "sorrowful, yet always rejoicing;

poor, yet making many rich; having nothing, and yet possessing everything."

Forgiveness doesn't mean we won't hurt. Instead, it means that feelings of anger and resentment will no longer have a foothold in our lives. It opens us up to being thankful to the Lord for what He has done in our own hearts and what He teaches us through forgiveness. In both cases where a friend and an acquaintance devastated me with their words, I am now able to thank the Lord. Through these situations, I've gained a greater awareness of all that God has forgiven me.

Closing the Door

Forgiveness many times can only come as we see the extent of forgiveness God grants us—daily. I am reminded in Colossians 3:13, "Bear with each other and forgive whatever grievances you may have against one another. Forgive as the Lord forgave you."

I have a friend who has struggled for years over the fact that her parents have never loved her. "Why do parents have children when they are going to hate them?" she once asked me. Every time she got together with her parents, all the old hurts returned.

For this friend, the breakthrough came one day when she wrote out every sin she could remember committing, including "hating my mother for hating me." Then across that list she wrote in bold red letters, "Forgiven by Jesus Christ." Next, she wrote a letter to her mother expressing all the hurts she endured, all the pain she felt. It took her an entire day to write the letter and she cried her way through it. She then took the red pen again and wrote boldly across the letter, "I forgive you as Christ has forgiven me." She took these two letters out to her backyard and buried them.

"This is a dead issue," she said. "Christ has forgiven me, and I forgive my mom. This is the end of it." Her ritual was freeing, however at times she does return to her yard and stand over the burial spot. Though forgiveness was granted, the hurt causes her to return from time to time and remember that, though she has been sinned against, her own sin toward God was greater, and He still was able to forgive her.

Forgiveness is never easy, but as my friend can attest, having wrestled with forgiveness of her parents for so long, it does get easier. "Because my walk with the Lord is growing and my focus is more readily set on Jesus, forgiveness gets easier with practice and perseverance." We need to continue to make the right choice—the choice to forgive—for we know the rewards of doing so are great.

Make It Happen

1. Like Carole's friend, consider writing out all the wrongs you feel have been done against you by someone you must forgive. Then write out all the wrongs you have done against the Lord. With bold, red letters write across the first list "I forgive you as Christ forgave me." Then across your own list write "Forgiven through Christ."

2. Consider doing a study of forgiveness based on the David Augsburger books *Freedom From Forgiveness* (Moody) or *Caring Enough to Forgive* (Regal Books).

3. Realize that forgiveness is not a feeling, but instead a willful decision to clear the record of wrongs against you by another person. Resist the temptation to act on your emotions when it comes to hurts and disappointments in a relationship. Instead, ask for God's grace that you might be able to rise above the emotions involved and offer forgiveness—the same kind of forgiveness offered us through Christ.

4. Sometimes we can't see the bitterness in our hearts. As Jeremiah 17:9 says, "The heart is deceitful above all things and beyond cure. Who can understand it?" Seek the counsel of a godly, older woman who won't be afraid to say, "I sense some bitterness in you." Take her observations seriously and encourage her to help you keep your heart on track with what God desires for your life.

Forgiving Our Debtors
Michelle Halseide

Unforgiveness is like fat in our spiritual arteries—it clogs the channel in which the Holy Spirit flows. The reason is simple. A bitter heart cannot worship a merciful God. An unforgiving spirit cannot commune with One who is so forgiving. Here's how to make forgiveness real in your life.

Reassess Your Right

Grudges like to grab us. We're easy prey because we're so preoccupied with justifying our rights and feelings. Before we can forgive offenses, a change of attitude must take place. We must first surrender our right to harbor a grudge, even if it can be justified on moral or legal grounds. Grudges are weapons—tools we use to get even, seek revenge, or punish our offenders. When we insist on the right to remain angry and resentful, we're asking God to condone sin—the sin of wanting someone else to suffer.

By contrast, when we give up our demands for justice, fairness, and kind treatment, we're obeying Christ's command to do what is *not* our duty—to go the second mile, to turn the other cheek, to love our enemies.

Resolve to Forgive

It's possible to forgive even when we don't feel like it. Jesus taught that forgiveness is neither an emotion, nor a change of heart, but an act of the will. Forgiving is not an option; it's our duty and responsibility. On the flip side, if we don't forgive, God can't deal with our negative emotions. Jesus said, "If you do not forgive men their sins, your Father will not forgive your sins" (Matthew 6:15).

Jesus was not implying our salvation is in jeopardy if we withhold forgiveness. Instead, He was implying that God will set us free from hurt and destructive feelings—our sin of unforgiveness—only when we release those who have wronged us.

Forgive Your Offenders

Sometimes we make the actual act of forgiving more difficult than necessary by loading it with extras. Forgiving is *not* overlooking, excusing, justifying, or whitewashing a wrongdoing. Nor is it understanding, analyzing, or accepting an offender's needs or motives. Forgiving is *not* taking the blame, denying your hurt, or asking God to forgive you of your bitterness. Nor is it changing feelings about a hurtful event, forgetting it, or even reconciling a relationship—although reconciliation often follows.

When God asks us to forgive a debtor, He means, *Follow my example—go on record and say: "I will not remember your sins"* (Isaiah 43:25, NASB). The act of forgiving is a promise to *not* remember an offense. It is not a passive response. Not remembering is something we can do.

Promising to not remember is another way of saying I will not bring up these matters to you or others in the future. I refuse to keep score or use your sins against you. I may not forget this offense completely, but I'm going to hurl your sins into the depths of the seas, just as God does for me (Micah 7:19).

Seek Reconciliation

The ultimate goal of forgiveness is not inner healing, but reconciliation. That's why God gave us a model for repairing damaged relationships. "If your brother sins against you, go and show him his fault, just between the two of you," Jesus taught (Matthew 18:15). Note that we are commanded to confront wrongdoers. So, whenever possible, clear the air.

—From *Today's Christian Woman* (November/December 1991)

14
Can I Be Angry With God?

—Carole Mayhall

WHEN MY GRANDSON, Eric, was three, my daughter taught him a saying about the unfairness of life. Whenever something unjust happened to him, Eric would say, "Life is harsh and unjust, but Jesus loves me, and He will take care of me." We all picked up on his saying, not simply because it was cute to hear him repeat it in his little three-year-old voice, but because it was absolutely true. Life *is* harsh and unjust, but Jesus loves us and will take care of us.

When life is unfair, when circumstances aren't going as we would like, we sometimes respond with anger toward God. I doubt there is one of us who hasn't at some time experienced this unsettling reaction. Yet, we wonder, can we be angry with God?

The answer is yes. Just as the Lord loves us and takes care of us, He understands our anger as well. However, I didn't fully realize this until my sister Joye was diagnosed with acute lymphatic leukemia.

After the diagnosis, doctors estimated Joye had four weeks to live, but God intervened and gave her two years. During her remarkable remission she was able to travel and witness to so many people that I could see why the Lord gave her extra time.

But then, in the final nine months of her life, the leukemia went into her brain, which caused it to swell in her skull. I watched Joye endure excruciating pain. Watching her suffer was almost unbearable. What made this time so trying for me wasn't so much that the Lord was going to take her, but instead that she would have to suffer so much before going to heaven.

Throughout this time, one part of me said, "Lord, I can't get through a day without your strength and help," which He readily gave. Yet, subconsciously, another part of me was angry with Him. I wanted to shake a fist at God and say, "How can you do this terrible thing? If you can allow such awful pain in a child of yours who loves you so much, then, just keep your distance."

Several times in those final months, Joye's health plummeted and I was called back to Michigan where I'd sit with her day after day. She rallied many times, but I was fairly certain God would allow me to be with her when she was taken to heaven.

As the days passed, though, I realized I might not be by her side when she died. Jack and I were scheduled to take a seven-week overseas ministry trip that was two years in the planning. Yet two weeks before we were to leave, my brother-in-law called and said, "She's dying. Come quick. It's really bad." Again, I felt sure I would be there when God took her home, but again she held on. The doctor said it could be a day, a week—he had no idea.

Joye wanted me to go on the trip. Jack wanted me to go. And I knew God wanted me to go, but *I* didn't want to go.

Everything was rebelling within me. I wanted so desperately to stay and be there for Joye, but the day came when I had to leave. I knew when I walked out of Joye's room it would be for the last time.

I gave her a hug. She rose from her semi-conscious state and we prayed together. I told her to hug Mom and Dad when she got to heaven and then I walked out of her room.

As I boarded the plane headed for home I was full of

anger. I couldn't believe God would allow her to go through so much pain and, on top of that, not allow me to be with her when she died. I felt as though my insides had shattered into a million pieces. Inside, I was screaming at God. "Where are you, God?" I asked. "I'm supposed to minister to others? What a joke! I have nothing to give. I am totally empty inside."

As the plane flew high above the clouds, God put one word into my heart—let. "Let?" I screamed inside. "What do you mean 'let?'" And God answered, "*Let* me heal you."

And suddenly, I realized at that moment what I'd been doing. Part of me was saying, "Lord, I can't get through one day without you," while another part was saying, "I'm mad at you so keep your distance."

Finally, I said, "Lord, I let." With those words a healing balm soothed my soul. Then all the "let" verses I had ever memorized started to wash over me.

"Let us then approach the throne of grace with confidence, so that we may receive mercy and find grace to help us in our time of need" (Hebrews 4:16). "Let the peace of Christ rule in your hearts, since as members of one body you were called to peace" (Colossians 3:15). "Let the word of Christ dwell in you richly as you teach and admonish one another with all wisdom, and as you sing psalms, hymns and spiritual songs with gratitude in your hearts to God" (Colossians 3:16). "Do not let your hearts be troubled. Trust in God, trust also in me" (John 14:1).

Verse after verse rushed over my spirit, and the millions of pieces inside of me came together as Christ spoke peace. His initial healing had begun.

Two weeks later, as Jack and I were about to travel from Germany to Ghana, West Africa, our daughter called with the news that Joye had died. However, my heart was at peace. The day of Joye's memorial service, Jack and I were ministering in Ghana and I could do so with a smile on my face. It didn't mean the hurt wasn't there. But in my heart, I no longer was angry with God.

Let It All Out

Somewhere in my upbringing I acquired the idea that as a Christian I should never ask "why." Yet on the cross Christ asked why. "Why have you forsaken me?"(Mark 15:34).

My experience with Joye made me realize that God could handle my "why" questions. He might not always answer them, but it's much healthier for us to go before the Lord and rant and rave like I did on the airplane, than to hold it inside or deny our feelings.

KEEPING THE LINES OPEN

When I am angry I keep talking to my heavenly Father so He can help me link into His power, peace, and grace in the midst of the turmoil around me. Then He gives me insights into how I should behave or how I can help or serve in the very set of circumstances in which I have angrily reacted in the first place. Accepting the things I cannot change comes first—then the anger goes and I'm open to receive His power to serve in the situation.

—Jill

Look at how King David repeatedly vents his frustrations in the Psalms with complaints like, "Lord, I feel like you've deserted me. Where in the world are you? I feel like the world is crushing around me, and I don't even see you in this." Yet, despite his honest emotional release, David always said, "But, I will still trust in you."

Once God revealed to me the anger I was feeling, I realized I needed to keep short accounts before Him. My anger over Joye's illness lasted about six months to a year. Before her illness, I was quick to say, "Lord, there is no fairness in this whatsoever." Now, I'm much quicker to say, "Lord, this doesn't seem fair, but I will still trust in you whether or not you show me *why*."

Be Angry, But Sin Not

It helps to have a friend that you're accountable to who can detect unspoken anger. She may notice that you lack a sense of joy. After all, you can't be angry and joyful at the same time. When you deny the emotion of anger, often you begin to lose all emotion.

Not long ago, Jack and I met with a couple. The wife sat there with tears streaming down her face while her husband sat beside her with his arms crossed, appearing very detached from the conversation.

"Two years ago we lost our only son in a terrible tractor accident on our farm. He had graduated with honors from high school and was about to enter college," she explained. "His death destroyed both of us. Now, two years later, it continues to destroy us because my husband will not talk about it. He has never talked about it. He will not enter into a conversation with me. He has totally denied his emotions."

To cope, this man had turned into a zombie of sorts. He thought that by not allowing his emotions to surface, by not experiencing his feelings of anger and pain, he'd be able to get through life.

There is a difference between numbness and denial. In the month following Joye's death, a numbness descended upon me that I didn't understand. Not only didn't I empathize with others in pain, but the emotions of joy, delight, spontaneity, even excitement from discoveries in God's Word were lacking in my life. My life became monotone and it scared me. Gradually, I realized God was protecting my emotions until they had a chance to heal. It was as though He had formed scar tissue around my damaged and fragile emotional nerve endings to protect them from further damage. When I realized that, I relaxed, and sure enough, little by little, I began to feel again.

Denial is another thing entirely. When I deny my pain, my anger, or the trauma I've gone through, and determine to stoically get through each day, I deny what makes me *me*. I become incapable of feeling any emotions—good or bad. It is impossible to shut down one part of our emotional self without the others being affected.

For example, try as I might, I never can fool Jack if I'm upset with him. Without me even saying a word, he knows that I'm upset or angry. And until I voice my anger and we talk things out, life isn't the same. There is a distance, a stiltedness in our communication, and I hate it!

Even more, I can't fool God. It's ridiculous to think that I can hide how I feel from the one who made me and knows what I think before I even think it! Trying to deny or ignore my anger never works. Until I come before the Lord with my anger, my joy, and my delight, my communication with Him is affected whether I acknowledge it or not.

Which Road to Travel

Ephesians 4:26 reads, "In your anger do not sin: Do not let the sun go down while you are still angry." This verse underscores two important facts about anger. First, it acknowledges we can expect to experience anger. Second, and most crucial, is that it's what we do with our anger that counts.

In most relationships we will become angry at some point. We've all felt irritated with a spouse we dearly love, or agitated by a close friend's behavior. Anger can drive you to sin—you could tell off your spouse or undermine a friend—or anger can draw you closer if you

172

work through it together. Likewise, our anger at God can cause us to sin. We can close off communication with Him and let our relationship wither. But if we acknowledge our anger and are willing to let the Lord deal with it, we'll come out the other side knowing a bit more of His wonderful, constant love and, in the process, love Him even more.

UNCHANGING CHARACTER

You can be angry with God—you can be anything you want with God and it will never alter His character or His promises to you. To be angry may represent a lack of faith, but to stay angry or to allow that anger to control you is sin.

—Kay

For instance, when I realized the extent of my anger with God over what Joye endured, I was amazed that throughout the ordeal, God's patience and love for me never faltered. He kept right on loving me. He didn't remove His hand of blessing on the ministry Jack and I were involved in. He continued to give me special insights from His Word. He gave me the strength to do what needed to be done. He even sent many sunbeams of delight through the dark clouds of my painful situation.

When I realized how great my subconscious anger had been, I understood even more how loving and patient my Father had been with me. As a result, I fell in love with Him all over again. But none of this could have happened had I kept my anger bottled up. I would have missed the often-needed reminder that God loves me despite my actions—that I can't earn His love.

Putting the Word to Work

As our relationship matures and our knowledge of God grows, we will become more sensitive to the times we do feel anger toward Him. As we read the Word and study it, we can trust that God will put His finger on those areas of our lives that need work. Often these areas will reveal themselves through anger over circumstances and may take other forms such as depression or discouragement. But just how do we open that line for God to talk to us—to show us our anger or frustration and help us move beyond it?

During my days in Portland, I was shown a personal application tool that helped me take the truths I learned as I studied the Bible out of the theoretical and into the practical. This tool has probably been the greatest method for allowing God to speak directly to me.

First, as I study my Bible, I stay alert for those little nudges from God—those times He says, "See this passage, it's just for you." Then, I write that passage down in my own words as I understand it. Next, I write down how I failed to obey that passage. I give a specific incident of where I failed to apply that verse. Last, I pray about how God wants me to apply that passage to my life in the coming week, and, if possible, I ask someone to check up on me to see if I have carried out my commitment. Children love to hold us accountable, but I have found it best to ask a friend or a member of a Bible study group to hold me accountable. The verse may be about handling anger or your temper, but whatever verse God gives you, if you use this tool the truth will become part of your life.

The first time I applied this tool was when my daughter was young. The verses I used were 1 Thessalonians 5:16–18, which read, "Be joyful always; pray continually; give thanks in all circumstances, for this is God's will for you in Christ Jesus." Initially, I skipped right over these verses. *It's impossible to be thankful all the time*, I thought. But I applied the tool I just described with some surprising results.

To me the verses said, "Give thanks in everything." I knew I didn't. In fact, I specifically remembered not giving thanks when my young daughter pulled a bucket of paint off a chair and spilled it all over herself, the floor, and the chair. Thinking back, I thought I was doing good by not flipping out and losing my temper. But I knew I really hadn't remained thankful even when the paint spilled.

So I resolved to memorize this verse so God could use it the next time I didn't want to give thanks, and I vowed that no matter what happened that day, I was going to say "Thank you, Lord" until living this verse became a habit and a way of thinking. What I was studying in my Bible was now changing my thinking patterns.

As you use this tool, remember to give yourself a cut-off point. For one week, you'll make a concentrated effort to follow God's Word—to take that particular verse to heart. But if you don't set a cut-off point soon you'll be working on fifty-two different verses all at once. That's impossible, and Satan will defeat you. Instead, have faith that God will lead you each week to the area you need to work on and do so with a willingness to obey.

———— ∽ ————

Mark 4:35–41 tells the story of Christ calming the waters and speaking peace to the storm. My experience with Joye's suffering and death was a tidal wave in my life. I was much like the disciples who said to Christ as they felt the waves break over the boat, "Teacher, don't you care if we drown?"

Whether we want to admit it or not, everyone of us at some time has said to God, "Don't you care? Don't you see what I'm going through? Don't you know?"

But how patient Christ was with His disciples and is with me. He didn't say, "I'm through with you." Instead,

He asked, "Why are you so afraid? Do you still have no faith?"

He calmed the sea for His disciples. He healed the broken pieces of my heart with the word "let." God cannot only accept and handle our anger but, if we let Him, He can speak peace to the turmoil in our souls.

Make It Happen

1. Study yourself. What behaviors surface when you're angry? Look for those hidden signs of anger like being short with family members, an inner feeling of unrest, or a decrease in compassion toward friends and co-workers. As you know yourself better, and see these hidden clues surface, make a dedicated effort to get to the root of your feelings. Ask yourself questions as simple as "Am I angry?" "Why am I mad?" Be honest with your answers. Share your concerns openly with God, asking for His help in uncovering the source of your anger.

2. If you are struggling with anger toward God, write Him a letter. Pour out your feelings, your frustrations, your outrage. Crumple up your letter and surrender it to God. Ask for His help in dealing with your anger. Read Psalm 13 or 25 and meditate on what it means to trust in the Lord no matter what your current circumstances.

3. Don't let your anger become a barrier between you and God. Realize it's our human tendency when we're angry to withdraw and allow a hurt to fester. Continue your daily disciplines of prayer and studying the Word even though you may feel you're being two-faced. Have confidence that the Lord can handle your anger and will help you work through it if you keep the lines of communication open.

4. Remember—God is on your side. If you ask for bread, He doesn't give you a stone. If circumstances in your life seem unfair, try to look at your life from God's

perspective. He is a loving father who wants the best for His children. The difficult times you may be going through now are God's way of preparing you for what He has planned next in your life.

PART THREE

UNDERSTANDING MY MINISTRY

BY THE VERY NATURE of our relationship with a living Lord we are called to move beyond our comfort zones to the world at large. In Matthew 28 we are called to "make disciples of all nations." In Hebrews 10 we are reminded not to abandon the habit of meeting regularly with fellow believers. In Luke 14:13–14 we are told, "But when you give a banquet, invite the poor, the crippled, the lame, the blind, and you will be blessed."

No, our faith is not something we tuck away and secretly nurture. Instead, it is something we are commanded to live out openly. Yet, while we know we are each called to serve the world, making our ministry more than talk doesn't always come naturally or easily. We get stumped by the politics of the church, shy in our witnessing, and overwhelmed by a world that grows more needy each day.

But we can take heart and meet the challenge to find and excel in our ministry. As Jill and Kay remind us, it is most often a combination of practice, patience, and dedication to living out our faith that finally allows the many pieces of our individual ministries to fall into place for the glory of our Lord.

15

Is It Essential for Me to Be Part of a Church?

—Jill Briscoe

IF YOU HAD ASKED Stuart and me early in our ministry if church was essential for a Christian we would have said, "No." Stuart was raised in a very strict church structure and was fed up with it. Even when he started his career in lay preaching he didn't rate wanting to be part of a church very high on his priority list. So together we preached to the street kids in England, confident we didn't need the church. After all, the church didn't understand the kids and what we hoped to do with them. Added to that was the fact the kids didn't really like the church, so we kept the two separated.

Then one day, someone asked Stuart, "How can you have such a low view of the church?" Stuart responded, "I'm all for Christ, but not for His church." This person's next words literally turned our lives around. "How can you be all for Christ and not all for what Christ is all for?"

Stuart began to study what the Bible said about the church and saw that the church was Christ's bride. Our choice to ignore the church was an insult to the bride of Christ. And if we claimed to be a member of Christ's body, how could we say we had no need of the other members of the body? It was like a hand running off by

183

itself. Stuart and I were spiritually out of sync in wanting to be mavericks, to do our own thing apart from the body of believers.

As Stuart further studied and taught the Scriptures, he came to these conclusions: We needed to be in a body. He needed to be a pastor. We needed to relocate to America. This is how Stuart became senior pastor of a church in Wisconsin. We are still here twenty-two years later!

What Is the Church?

In my mind, the church is best described as a living organism—not so much a building or a corporation as we are sometimes in the habit of viewing the church. One of my favorite quotes of Stuart's describes the church best. According to him, "Church is not somewhere you go. It's something you are. You're a member of a mystical body that meets in a visible, material place." I couldn't agree with him more. And when we choose to view the church from this perspective, we're much more likely to have positive experiences within it and good feelings about it.

THE CALLED ONES

When you become a Christian, you don't join an organization. You become a member of the church of the living God, part of the *ecclesia*—His called-out ones. The church is never described in the Word as an organization or as an inorganic structure. First Peter 2 says the church is a dwelling of living stones built on the foundation stone of the Lord Jesus Christ. When you become a child of God, you become part of God's forever family—bone of His bone, a member of His body.

—Kay

In Hebrews 10:25 we are told, "Let us not give up meeting together, as some are in the habit of doing, but let us encourage one another—and all the more as you see the Day approaching." We are mandated to assemble together, and it is this assembly that forms the church. If we choose to be outside of the church then we will end up living outside the full realm of blessings God has called us to enjoy—and one of those blessings is the fellowship of believers.

I once read a definition of fellowship as "two fellows in a ship." When the ship is afloat, you both are buoyed up. When it goes down, you both go down. The church is a place where people can bear each other's burdens—go up and down together. That's what fellowship is all about. And the church is the best environment for that to happen.

For instance, I've seen the blessing of fellowship and friendship at work in our church. We have a food pantry, and nearly every Sunday morning I see teams of people working to prepare food baskets. In the process of serving the Lord, many of these folks have become good friends. As a team they bag the groceries and deliver them to the inner city. At times they even stay and prepare a meal. As they drive to deliver the food, and on the return trip home, these teams pray for those they are able to serve. And what's more, these servants can't wait until the next Sunday to repeat the whole process. These people would miss out on such wonderful blessings if they chose not to be part of a church—a body of believers committed to service and fellowship.

When We'd Rather Go Solo

At some point in our life, we will likely be put off by church. It might seem hypocritical, dull, or lacking in opportunities to grow spiritually. However, before we declare, "Church isn't for me," we need to realize the reason for our dissatisfaction isn't the church but, instead, it stems from members of the body who are not functioning as they should. Even Jesus, early in His ministry, experienced a dead church when He returned to Nazareth. Those at the church were furious at His attempt to minister to them and even went so far as to try to push Him off a cliff!

When you feel negative about church, take a moment to check your automatic response and write it off. Declaring church hypocritical makes no more sense than refusing to seek medical care because you once went to a doctor who was a quack. Medical care is a necessity, just as the church is a necessity for a believer. Just because some believers don't shape up, this shouldn't be an excuse to say church isn't for you.

FOCUS ON THE PERFECT

If we see hypocritical people in the church we should first pray for those people. After all, hypocrisy by definition means pretending to be what one is not, and in light of that definition, I'm sure we would all stand guilty before God at some point in our lives. To help me keep the hypocrisy I might encounter from derailing me I try to focus on the perfect Christ rather than on imperfect man. Also, we have to watch that we don't put people on pedestals, because when their lives collapse, our faith can collapse as well.

—Carole

My father attended a small evangelical church before the second world war. After the war, however, he never returned to a fellowship. Consequently, I never grew up in church. It was not until my father's funeral that his sister—my aunt—told me that there had been a big row in that particular body of believers, which had been so bitter my father had left, vowing never to return. And he didn't. Even today, I hear similar stories over and over.

Gauge Those Expectations

Our discontentment with the church can arise from an unpleasant and negative experience with people or from a "me-oriented" attitude. This "what's in it for me?" attitude has pervaded our family life, our work ethic, and, sadly, our involvement in God's church.

Some time ago, a family expressed interest in joining our fellowship. Stuart met with the family, and the first question the father asked was, "What does your church have to offer my family?"

"Before I answer that, what does your family have to offer our church?" asked Stuart. "You won't be happy in our church fellowship unless you come with that attitude." The family never did come. It's just as well because they never would have found contentment. When we get over, "what has the church got to offer me?" and get around to, "what do I have to offer the church," then our involvement will begin to have meaning. Once we can make this shift, then we will receive all the church has to offer.

A lot of people spend a lot of time searching for a church that meets their needs. That church will never exist. There is no perfect church, and if there is, don't join it. As Billy Graham says, "You'll spoil it."

———— ❦ ————

One criticism I hear from time to time regarding the church is that the pastor's sermons are dull, short on application, or don't meet a felt spiritual need. Now, I think it's a fair expectation for the pastor's sermons to speak to us. However, they won't unless we do some work beforehand.

Most often, as we sit in the pew on Sunday morning,

we are surrounded with baggage. We don't expect to be blessed. We don't think much of the pastor's skills. We criticize this and that. Unless we leave the baggage at home, we won't realize our expectations for Sunday morning worship.

I've learned to go to church expecting to hear God's voice through my pastor. Take a notebook and a pencil, and ask God before you go, "Speak to me." Listen for God's voice, and you will never, ever go away disappointed.

Now, it's not always easy to go expecting to hear God's voice. Believe me, I know. I get to listen to my husband, who, for that hour on Sunday morning, becomes my shepherd and pastor. At times it is a challenge for me to hear God's voice through my husband because I know him as he is. I don't mean that negatively, but rather, I know him as a husband, as a lover, and as a friend. Yet, during times of worship, he is the one through whom God will speak to me. Although it is a challenge to clear my mind for worship, I'm able do so because I've learned to say, "Today I believe I'm going to hear the voice of God." I take my notebook, and I sit at the front of the sanctuary, not because I want to be noticed, but because I want to be attentive to what God is trying to say to me.

One final thing that can cause our expectations to be less than realistic for the church is, surprisingly, all the polished and professional Christian radio and other sophisticated ministries. Take, for example, some of the incredible guest speakers at women's retreats, or the professional video tapes often used for classroom teaching.

While there is nothing inherently wrong with these ministries—in fact they play an important role in the lives of many Christians—they have raised our expectations to the point where nothing less than the "best" will do. We expect to be entertained rather than to participate in worship. We expect to come away feeling awed and uplifted by a well-orchestrated hour of worship that we have "owned" and enjoyed.

The problem is a perfect hour of worship rarely occurs in the local church. And when a top-notch performance is our expectation, poor Pastor Jones and his small church of 100, with Mrs. Smith at the piano and Bob teaching Ephesians, can't compete.

In a way, we're doing ourselves a disservice because we rely too much on packaged and polished expertise instead of encouraging the local body of believers to discover the gifts they have and minister to each other. For instance, right now I have the opportunity to prepare a video series of my work that's suitable for Sunday school use—but I hesitate to follow through for this very reason. Will the use of my tapes displace someone within the local church who has the potential gift to teach? I'm still searching my heart on this issue.

Turning Disappointment Into Hope

The main reason we should attend church is for the opportunity to listen to what God has to say to us and to worship Him. Several months ago, a young woman in her thirties shared with me how frustrated she was with church and how it hadn't met her expectations of a place to make friends and enjoy fun and fellowship.

She told me, "One night, as I was again complaining to my husband about how disappointed I was with church, I suddenly asked him, 'Why do you go to church?' His answer was simple. He said, 'I go to worship.'"

This woman realized she wanted all the fringe benefits of church involvement, and in her quest for those she had completely missed the real reason we are part of a body of believers.

"I'm rethinking my approach to church," she admitted to me. "No longer do I have a long list of expectations—that only leads to frustration. Instead, I'm trying to focus on worshiping God, and it's so liberating."

———— ∞ ————

There is one expectation we should always hold on to. We should expect to belong to a church that is true to the Scriptures and preaches the Gospel. We should be able to expect the body of believers to adhere to a common creed that agrees with what we've read in our Bible. And then we need to take it from there. Sure, the church you choose may not be perfect. But walk in with the attitude, "This is a Bible-based church and it is the best available. Now, let me see how I can make it better."

There are so many churches in the United States that are lively enough to satisfy the needs of my family. On the other hand, I could take you to Europe and we could visit city after city and not find one church as good as those we have here in the States. In fact, there are whole parts of the world that don't even have any churches.

Satan hates the bride of Christ—the Church—and he'll do everything he can to disrupt your commitment to her. Knowing this, do all you can to make church a positive experience—to let it be the blessing God intended it to be.

I've often thought of a church as a charcoal fire. When the coals are kept close together, they burn their brightest and give off an amazing glow. Together, they can do their job. And I've noticed how quickly a single coal can lose its warmth and glow, once it falls out of the fire. We are to be like those coals, huddled together to do Christ's work in this world.

Make It Happen

1. Write down *all* the expectations you have of church membership. Look them over carefully, then

rank them according to how realistic each expectation is. Be honest—should friendships rank above your desire to have a worshipful experience? Give your unrealistic expectations to God and ask that they not impede you from finding joy within the church.

2. Give yourself time with a church. If there is something you don't like, resist the temptation to complain to your friends or fellow members. Instead, do something. The body of Christ is a living organism not a stagnant mass. Where can you make changes? If you have feelings on a particular issue, without a doubt many others feel the same as you. Take the initiative to serve the church with a goal to make it stronger.

3. Read the book of Acts. What does it have to say about the early church? Compared to current day challenges the church faces, what is different and what is the same? How does reading this account of the early church change your understanding of what the church should be about?

4. If you don't currently belong to a church, take steps today to find and join a local body of believers. Church membership means much more than just attending—it means making a formal and public declaration of your commitment to a certain body of Christ.

16

How Can I Help a Needy World?

—Jill Briscoe

YEARS AGO, AS I WAITED in line at a local shop, I heard the gossip of the day. My neighbor's husband had left her. The night before, he had packed his things into a van and driven out of her life.

I knew my neighbor casually. When we did speak, which wasn't too often, it was about the weather or other inconsequential topics. Our subdivision was the type where everyone led his own life and neighbors didn't really get to know one another.

When I returned home from my errand, I struggled with what to do. Should I visit my neighbor or pretend I knew nothing about her situation and go on with my day? Yet, in my mind I could see her sitting at her kitchen table, alone. She was in her fifties and the kids were grown. Finally, I got up the courage and walked over to her house. When she opened her door, I said, "I heard through the grapevine your husband left you last night. Can I do anything to help?" She immediately burst into tears and said, "Come in. Come in." I spent the morning with her. All I did then was listen, put my arm around her, and have a cup of coffee. But it was the start of a relationship.

Sometimes when we think of a needy world we think of faraway places and large numbers of people in desperate circumstances, when in reality our needy world might be right next door.

Who Makes Up Your Multitude?

If we hope to help a needy world, we first must discover the needs God wants us to care for. Each day, if we just open our eyes, we are surrounded by a multitude of need.

Need isn't restricted to size. Just because you may not be led to serve 500 women doesn't mean you haven't contributed significantly. Don't let small numbers turn you off. Most often our multitude comes in more manageable sizes, like a single individual such as my neighbor. Sometimes the sheer number of problems one person has can make her a multitude of need at one time. I remember taking my eight-year-old son's face in my hands and calling him "my little multitude" because of the many needs he presented to me.

Jesus and His disciples hadn't been in ministry very long before they were met by great need. If we are sensitive to the needy as Jesus was, before long we will find places and people to serve. You can start by looking around your neighborhood and then within the community and other neighboring cities and towns. When Jesus and His disciples were preparing to feed the multitude of 5,000 on the shore of the Sea of Galilee, Jesus pulled Philip aside and asked him, "How will we feed these people?" Bethsaida was Philip's home town and Jesus was saying, in essence, "I hold you accountable and responsible for your own crowd. Who else could care for Bethsaida like you, Philip? Surely you will be the one who says we've got to feed them." Likewise, we will be held accountable for finding and helping the needy within our reach—within our own communities.

Finding Your Niche

The account where Jesus asks Philip this question is found in John 6:1–15. This story is one I'm certain many of us are familiar with—it tells of how Jesus performed a miracle to feed the masses with only five loaves of barley bread and two fish given to Him by a little boy.

Like Christ, we are to feed, or care for the needy. And in that crowd I'm sure there were many needy people—the newly divorced, the destitute, the skeptics—not much different from the crowd we face today. In Scripture we are told not to withhold what is in our power to do for the needy. Jesus tells us in Matthew 25:40, "I tell you the truth, whatever you did for one of the least of these brothers of mine, you did for me."

WHAT IS MOST PLEASING?

The single most important and significant thing you can do to help a needy world is to live a Christlike life before them—to determine to live and respond as your Savior did. He always did those things which pleased the Father—even the words He spoke were the Father's. Impossible? No, with Christ in you all things are possible. Press on, valiant one.

—Kay

But just how do we determine what specific need we are called to address? When I began my work in women's ministries, I came across a verse, Lamentations 3:51, "Mine eye affecteth mine heart because of all the daughters of my city" (KJV). Now, my heart was set on kids and that was where I wanted to minister. But as my eye took in what was happening in America, and as I began to look into the hearts and needs of women, "mine eye affecteth mine heart." God lent me the compassion He has for women, and that is where I found my needy multitude.

If you don't have compassion for a need, ask God to give you His heart for it. Those you are ministering to will know if you have a heart for them or not. And, as I discovered, only God can give you a heart for what He wants you to do.

This was certainly true in my case. The small neighborhood Bible class I started grew rapidly. Soon it expanded to a large ministry involving hundreds of women. As I spent time getting to know women and listening to their heartbeat, I felt my own heart strongly warmed toward them. Having become involved, I discovered myself concerned with the needs of widows, young mothers, battered women, and business women. Women of all shapes and sizes, all colors and creeds, haunted my heart and drove me to create opportunities for them to find the Lord and learn to serve Him. This wouldn't have been possible had the Lord not given me a heart for women.

When You Can't Do It All

The multitude of need that surrounds us daily can be overwhelming. And what we do may seem like so little in comparison to the enormous need we see. It pays to keep our outreach in perspective and, thankfully, Jesus gave an excellent example of how we are to view the little that we as individuals can do.

In Mark 14:3–11, while Jesus was in Bethany before the Passover, a woman came to Him with an alabaster jar of expensive perfume. She broke the jar and poured the perfume over His head. Some of those present were incensed that she had wasted the perfume. But Jesus praised the woman because "she did what she could."

We are never asked to do what we can't. The Lord certainly doesn't expect us to give as generously as a millionaire. If we have young children at home, He doesn't expect us to give the number of hours in the church or in the community that a retired woman might have available. What He does expect is for us to give what we can give. No good comes from comparing ourselves to others. What will come in some cases is a sense of guilt—only it's false guilt that comes from erroneous thinking.

I have suffered from guilt ever since I became a Christian. I have to admit, though, I seldom suffered from it before I became a Christian! Having the Holy Spirit in your life, however, does lay some heavy responsibilities and needs on your heart. I have always been invited to minister; to speak and give my testimony, to write, create, organize, and lead. I have never had to pray, "Lord, open a door." Rather, I have prayed He would close a few so I would know which opportunities of Christian service I should take. Yet, I've wrestled with guilt feelings when I don't try to go through every open door.

SETTING A COURSE

I'm not the most organized, goal-oriented person. I keep my goals in my head. However, when I have taken the time to spell them out on paper, it allows me to review them with someone who really knows me and see if I'm being realistic. Since I tend to overcommit, Jack helps me avoid this when he looks at my goals and asks questions like, "Is this opportunity going to detract from what's on your heart?"

—Carole

I know it's ridiculous to think I should say "yes" to each and every opportunity, but even knowing that doesn't seem to ease my guilt about saying "no." I have had to remind myself of what Jesus said, "My food is to do the will of him who sent me, and to accomplish his work" (John 4:34, Phillips). Jesus finished the work He had to do, then went home to heaven after a brief three-year ministry on earth. He did not finish anyone else's work—just His own. I must try to discern what is "my" work and then refuse to feel guilty when I say "no" to the responsibilities of others. The Holy Spirit, the Counselor-One who has come alongside to help, will guide me and convict me, letting me know when to say "yes" or "no."

To determine if it's true or false guilt ask yourself: *What am I doing about the needs I see? Am I doing enough according to my means? Am I doing what God expects me to do?* Then pray about it.

We shouldn't fear true guilt. In fact, I think there is such a thing as healthy guilt and it works much like our conscience. It can be a red alert. It may be what God is using to bring me back to Him and to the needs He wants me to meet. If you are feeling a sense of guilt, ask yourself, "Is this need something God wants me and me alone to meet? Is God giving me this burden?" Again, go before the Lord in prayer for the answer. Guilt is like pain. It's a built-in blessing that tells us something is wrong. Certainly we can't do everything, but we do need to be listening to God and following His call.

Stop, Help, and Go

Jesus and His disciples were hoping for a vacation of sorts when they got to Bethsaida. But instead of a respite, they were met with a crowd full of needy people. Our natural desire, as shown in Philip's words, is to send them away. Philip saw no possible way that, with the money available, Jesus and the disciples could feed such a large crowd.

Indeed, the needs of the multitude can become overwhelming. We can get "peopled out." I remember going on a vacation once and seeing a ministry team coming down the beach sharing Christ. I turned and ran in the opposite direction. I said, "This is my vacation."

But once again, Jesus showed His disciples how to respond. Even if meeting the needs of your multitude isn't on your agenda, you stop, help out, and then continue on. Christ operated on compassion and He was filled with compassion for this crowd. Yet, the disciples were engineering ways to disperse the crowd so they didn't have to feed so many.

We can't expect to have hours like the post office when it comes to meeting others' needs. And if we approach servanthood as a twenty-four-hour-a-day on-call duty, we won't be disappointed when a friend disrupts our plans for a relaxing evening at home, or a 7:00 A.M. call interrupts our tightly scheduled morning.

Giving Your Little to God

At the Sea of Galilee Jesus met the needs of the masses with little to begin with—a young boy's five loaves of barley bread and two fish. Similarly, we need to start with the little we have and trust that God will take care of the rest.

We must each hear the challenge of the needy and we must each decide how we will respond to it. But above all, we must acknowledge our total inadequacy in the face of such appalling needs in our world. We are asked to give our little to a big God and give it *all*. The little boy didn't just share his lunch with Jesus, he surrendered everything to Him. A miracle can happen when a little person like you or me gets together with a great big, adequate God who knows what He is going to do with what we have to offer.

God takes what we are willing to give and blesses it. And then He puts it to work to feed our hungry, needy world.

Make It Happen

1. Study the local newspaper or your church bulletin for needs within your community. Clip out those that catch your attention and are feasible for you based on

your time, talents, and money. Set aside some time one morning or evening to prayerfully bring before the Lord these needs. Ask for His help in determining which of the many needs that surround you will become your multitude.

2. If your desire is to meet needs on a more global level as well as a local level then consider becoming involved with a relief organization. Above all, tap into the literature these organizations provide so you can learn of the needs and how they can be met. Without knowledge of the needs, we can't do much.

3. Don't spend too much time planning how you'll help meet the needs of those around you. While planning has its virtues, it can also lead to inaction. If the Lord moves you to jump in, do it now!

4. Be realistic with what you can and can't do to help the needy. Our ministry of helping those in need is part of our job as Christ's ambassadors. Look for a balance in your life. Your dedication to serving each Saturday at the local food pantry may be admirable, but if it's negatively affecting your family then it is time to rethink how you should best use your God-given time and talents. Consider selecting a service to the needy that can be a family project.

Giving Back
Marita Littauer

God can use *you* to make a difference in the lives of others. Unfortunately, too many women think that in order for God to use them, they must be part of an organized ministry, have had a traumatic background, or be specially talented. Not true. The good news is that God can use you in whatever situation you are in today. And whether your personal ministry impacts many people or just a few, you'll find that giving back also makes a difference in *you*.

Each of us has been called to give back what God has given to us. Deuteronomy 16:17 says, "Every man shall give as he is able, according to the blessing of the Lord your God which he has given you" (NASB).

As you look at your own life experiences and resources, you may have an idea of what you could do to give back to others. But how can you tell if your ideas are God's plan for your personal ministry? Here are some steps to guide you:

Know God. If we want to hear God's voice, we first need to know Him. John 10:14, 16 says: "I am the Good Shepherd; I know my sheep and my sheep know me. They too will listen to my voice, and there shall be one flock and one shepherd."

There was a time in my life when I had accepted Christ but wasn't seeking His direction and guidance on how I could "give back" with my abilities. I had started my own color-analysis business, and things were going well. Then one day I got an idea to hold color-analysis seminars as a ministry outreach. My friend and I were going to lead them, and we thought it was a great idea. But God had other plans. He didn't bless our efforts and our seminars never grew beyond the freebies we did for demonstrations.

If you wish to start a personal ministry, first be sure you have a relationship with the Lord. He speaks softly, and you won't be able to hear His direction unless you are close to Him.

Pray continually. Romans 12:12 (TLB) tells us to be "prayerful always," yet when we observe Christ's life in Scripture, we see He wasn't constantly on His knees. He had work to do and He went about it daily. But Christ had an attitude of constant communion with His heavenly Father. He sought His Father's guidance in everything He did.

When Bonnie Skinner noticed some sad women in her office—single mothers with more burdens than they could bear alone—she asked God for help. It wasn't a formal prayer, but rather a sigh at her desk as part of her regular communion with God. She wasn't really looking for a personal ministry, but God gave her a plan to welcome the women into her home for weekend retreats. She had just redecorated and didn't want her lovely home messed up, but God persisted and Bonnie knew this was what she was supposed to do. Now she's had more than fifteen "mini-retreats" in her home.

Ask for specific direction. If you have an idea for a personal ministry, take that idea to God and ask for His direction. Is it really His plan for you or is it coming from some need for recognition? If you are still looking for a way you can give back, ask God. Ezekiel 36:37 tells us that "The Lord God says: I am ready to hear . . . and grant them their requests. Let them but ask . . ." (TLB).

Yvonne Martinez prayed for specific direction. As an adult child of divorce and a victim of rape, Yvonne spent several years in the healing process. When she was asked to share her story with some women, their lives were touched. Soon Yvonne was asked to share with a larger group. At the same time, Yvonne's church approached her to head up a support group for victims. She took the request to the Lord in prayer and asked specifically for guidance. The Lord opened all the doors and Yvonne began to turn her healing into helping. Many support groups later, Yvonne now spends much of her time teaching others how to lead support groups.

Wait for the Lord. Many of us today are accustomed to instant everything—fast food, speedy service. Waiting is not a welcome part of our lives. Yet it is often part of God's plan for us. Psalm 27:14 says: "Don't be impatient. Wait for the Lord . . . Yes, wait and he will help you" (TLB).

Once I finally let go of my color-analysis business, three years passed before God opened another door. I had to wait, but it was worth it. On the other side of the door, God had a more exciting opportunity for me.

Weigh your answer. When we *think* we have an answer to our prayers, it is important to *confirm* that answer with Scripture. If the Bible doesn't directly address the issue, seek wise counsel. I often find God doesn't call a young mother into a full-time speaking and traveling ministry while she has little ones at home. But it can be a wonderful time in her life for personal ministry to children in her neighborhood.

Thank God. Once God has confirmed the direction of our own personal ministry, we must thank Him. Philippians 4:6 sums it up perfectly: "Don't worry about anything; instead pray about everything; tell God your needs, and don't forget to thank him for his answers" (TLB).

—From *Today's Christian Woman* (January/February 1992)

17

How Can I Be More Confident Sharing My Faith?

—*Kay Arthur*

LATE LAST YEAR, I had the opportunity to teach at a large women's conference for the U.S. military forces in Europe. Because only a few knew anything of me, I felt the Lord prompt me to share my testimony.

I told of how I had wrestled with immorality before I was saved and how, despite being raised in a church, I had never heard the Gospel. I thought my baptism made me a child of God and my confirmation gave me the Holy Spirit. I didn't know that the reason I couldn't be good was because I was a sinner. I didn't know I needed to be saved. I didn't know my body was to be the temple of the Holy Spirit.

The next day at the bookstore women lined up to talk with me. I couldn't help but notice a woman who lingered on the periphery. She watched intently, and I was eager to talk with her. Finally her turn came. She took the chair opposite mine, leaned back, looked me in the eye and said, "I want you to know I'm not one of your kiss-up groupies."

"Well, good," I said, as I smiled and threw up a quick prayer for discernment.

"As a matter of fact," she said, leaning forward and propping her elbow on her crossed leg, "you really tick me off. You really think you're something, but you don't even understand the Word of God. It is perfectly all right for two people to sleep together, even though they're married to someone else, as long as they're consenting adults. You don't understand the meaning of the word 'adultery.' "

I smiled. I was excited because I felt that this was a divine appointment. As we talked, Linda, as I'll call her, told me that she was studying to be a lay chaplain, that she was a college graduate, had been to seminary, and had led various Bible studies. God was up to something. I listened and prayed. Periodically, I tried to counteract her arguments with Scripture but got nowhere. Finally, at the Lord's prompting, I leaned forward, looked her straight in the eye, and said, as gently and as lovingly as I could, "Linda, you're going to want to slug me for what I'm about to tell you, but I'll understand. You are deceived. You are going to hell. What you have is a religion and not a relationship. Your father is the devil. And my Father is God. You have no business being a lay chaplain; you don't know God."

She didn't slug me. As a matter of fact, she walked me to lunch, and I promised her we'd talk more later.

Two nights later she came to an extra session of mine that ran from 10:00 P.M. until midnight. Afterward, as we walked through the tunnel that led to the hotel she followed like a little puppy, wanting to argue some more. Finally I said, "Linda, it's so late. Why don't you just write me?"

Her response was instant, "We've got to talk tonight." We went back to my room and talked from 2:00 to 7:00 A.M.

Bit by bit, the details of her life came out. She and her husband were involved in a pornography ring and that was how they made their living. She was sleeping with a female chaplain during the conference while her husband was home sleeping with a mutual friend. In her mind it was okay in God's eyes because both she and her husband had consented to this kind of lifestyle. No wonder my teaching ticked her off!

As Linda picked up the argument she started two days ago, trying to convince me that I didn't understand the Bible, I said, "Read this." I took her from one passage to another in the Bible that spoke to the issue of immorality and its consequences. After reading each passage aloud, she'd say, "But . . ." to which I'd reply, "Don't argue with me. I didn't say it. Read this."

She faltered as she read Romans 1:26–27, "For this reason God gave them over to degrading passions, for their women exchanged the natural function for that which is unnatural . . . committing indecent acts and receiving in their own persons the due penalty of their error"(NASB).

Finally, I said, "You're arguing with me. Why don't we just get on our knees and talk to God about it. Your argument isn't with me—it's with God."

In a few minutes she was sobbing. The veil was coming off! She was seeing sin for what it was. In just a little while, she turned to me, mascara running down her cheeks, and said, "I feel so wicked, so desperately wicked."

She cried and prayed some more. At last, God had broken her. She was now in need of a Savior, and there on her knees she received the Lord Jesus Christ. We cried with joy and laughed as she told me how she had planned to set me straight that evening. Then we went to prayer again as she renounced the works of darkness and claimed the cleansing of the blood of her Jesus Christ.

My friend's life hasn't been easy since that moment. She's been beaten by her husband and locked out of her home, but she has stopped being immoral. As we talked later, discussing her future, she commented, "There's been so much garbage in my life. I need someone like you to disciple me—someone who will listen to me and love me yet not let me get away with anything. Someone who, like you, isn't afraid to call sin sin. I had others fooled, but I couldn't fool you."

———— ∽ ————

What is witnessing all about? It's simply letting sinners know "that Christ Jesus came into the world to save sinners" (1 Timothy 1:15, NASB). He didn't come to call the righteous; He came to call sinners to repentance, to a change of mind about sin. This is what the Gospel is all about! It's the good news that Jesus Christ's sacrifice sufficiently paid for every human being's sin once and for all. Those of us who truly know the Lord Jesus Christ know this truth. Yet, how can we be more confident in sharing this truth with others? After all, we are responsible to "preach the word; be ready in season and out of season" (2 Timothy 4:2, NASB). Romans 1:16 says that the Gospel is the power of God to salvation to everyone who believes. And in Luke 13 we read that unless people repent they are going to perish.

Linda, my precious new friend and my daughter in the Lord, had been on her way to hell and didn't even know it. She thought she was fine until she saw what the Word of God had to say.

When I began sharing with Linda, I didn't know if anything of eternal value would come from it. However, there are certain truths that give me the confidence I need in such situations. Let me share them with you.

Keys to Confidence

First, I knew that "faith comes from hearing, and hearing by the word of Christ" (Romans 10:17, NASB). According to *Vine's Expository Dictionary* the word for *word* in Greek is *rhema* which means a specific word, that which is uttered or spoken—a particular Scripture the Spirit brings to our remembrance for use in time of need. In the passage I just quoted, we see that faith comes from hearing the specific word concerning Christ. If we'll remember this, then it will give us confidence in sharing Him.

Witnessing is simply presenting to another individual the person and the work of our Lord Jesus Christ. The more intimately we know Him, the greater our understanding of His person and His work, the easier it will be to talk about Him to others. Christ is God in the flesh—the one who was tempted in every way that we have been but who did not yield to sin. He who knew no sin was made to be sin for us. He paid the penalty for our sin, and through the shedding of His blood we can have forgiveness of sins. There is no other way to salvation. He is the only way to God.

Jesus came for the express purpose of dying for our sin and, in dying, to set us free from slavery to sin. So often today we hear the Gospel "sold" as what Christ can do for us. He's going to make us happy. He's going to take care of all our problems. He becomes a cosmic Santa Claus instead of the one who delivers us from our sin. Maybe you lack confidence in "sharing your faith" because you're not presenting Jesus Christ for who He really is. He didn't come to make us happy. He came to make us holy! And without holiness no man will see God (Hebrews 12:14).

———— ✐ ————

The second key to confidence in witnessing is to realize I am not sharing "my" faith. Often we hesitate to share our faith with others because we don't feel we have our act together spiritually. We think, "What do I have to share?" or "Who am I to talk?"

What freezes us in our tracks is the pronoun "my." If we realize what we're sharing is the Gospel of Jesus Christ instead of our own personal experiences, we have a great deal to share. It is the Gospel that has the power to bring salvation—not my testimony or experience, not my faith, not my technique.

For instance, when I share my testimony, I talk about my past as an immoral woman but only as a platform for the truth that Christ came into this world to save sinners. As I share "my" testimony, I constantly intersperse it with Scripture to show what God has to say. Remember, faith comes by hearing the Word concerning Christ, not concerning me! If you'll remember that your testimony is not the Gospel, but a vehicle for sharing the Gospel, it will help a great deal.

JUST DO IT

Confidence in sharing your faith comes through practice. Share and your confidence will grow. Start to talk about your relationship with God more at home with family and friends. Join a Bible study or prayer group where verbal participation is encouraged. Pray for one unbeliever—make contact, spend time with her expecting an opportunity to open up. Do it!

—Jill

A third source of confidence is the realization that witnessing is really the work of the Holy Spirit. Acts 1:8 contains a promise from the Lord to His disciples that the Holy Spirit will come to dwell in them so they can be witnesses for Him. The disciples would not become orphans when Christ went away, but rather God would send a helper—the Holy Spirit, who would convict the world "concerning sin, and righteousness, and judgment" (John 16:7–11, NASB).

Witnessing is simply making one's self available to the Spirit to do His work. I followed the Spirit as I dealt with Linda. The pressure is off when we realize witnessing is not "sharing my faith," but rather allowing the work of the Holy Spirit within us and through us!

Time to Convict

When I present the Gospel, I must remember the Gospel is for sinners. I've got to allow God time to convict a person of his sin. Often we either whitewash sin or push for a decision that hasn't been made based on a conviction of sin.

We don't want to hold someone to the line and see them go through what Linda went through. Personally, I feel the reason we have so many professions of faith and so few transformed lives is because we shared "our faith" but forgot to deliver the Gospel. We don't allow a person to see his sin, realize his total impotence to be free from it, and then recognize that deliverance can only come through faith in the Lord Jesus Christ.

———— ✐ ————

Another vital truth to remember as we witness—one we often forget or ignore—is that when we witness we are declaring war on the powers of darkness. When God saved and commissioned Paul, He told him, "I am sending you to open their eyes so that they may turn from darkness to light and from the dominion of Satan to God, in order that they may receive forgiveness of sins and an inheritance among those who have been sanctified by faith in me" (Acts 26:17–18, NASB).

When I witness, I set out to free others from Satan's dominion. Knowing this I can expect warfare. The warfare will usually be subtle—attacking me or the person to whom I am witnessing. The attacks can be in the form of worry over how I'll present the Gospel. It might be fear that someone will respond negatively or think less of me as I share with her. It might be a running dialogue in my mind that says, "You don't need to share with this person." If I recognize I'm in warfare and understand that I'm invading Satan's territory, I can be prepared for his attacks. When the forces of the enemy come toward me, I can stand against them with prayer and God's Word.

211

———— ∞ ————

The Christian's one and only offensive weapon against the enemy is the "sword of the Spirit, which is the word of God" (Ephesians 6:17, NASB). Since faith comes by hearing the Word and since the Word of God is the sword of the Spirit, you can have great confidence in witnessing if you will use the Word of God. The Word was what broke, then convicted Linda and set her free. She had to *hear* the truth. She had to *read* the truth.

Know God's Word. I've seen people give a moving and exciting testimony, yet because the Word of God was not present the message lacked saving power. Don't move people to decisions on the basis of emotions! Share truth and allow the Word to do its work!

Whenever I share the Gospel, I ask God what Scriptures, what truths I need to share with that person. Then I keep hammering those verses home, knowing that if the person does not respond immediately, God will bring those verses back to mind at some later time. I have had people say to me, "I couldn't get those verses out of my mind."

Also, if opportunity allows, I always try to have the person to whom I'm witnessing read the Word of God aloud. Hearing the words of God as they come out of your own mouth can be very convicting.

Tools of the Trade

As we go about sharing the Gospel message, we have several tools and tactics at our disposal. The first is gentleness, which I learned a long time ago from another Bible teacher, Elizabeth MacDonald. While I witness out of obedience, Elizabeth has the gift of evangelism. I'll never forget watching Elizabeth as she took off her little half-glasses, reached over, patted a woman's hand, and lovingly said, "Honey, you are going to hell." Elizabeth was able to say that sentence so sweetly and with such compassion, the person she addressed couldn't get mad at her.

In my earlier days, I wouldn't have been that gentle or compassionate. Yet, through watching Elizabeth, I learned you can say almost anything to anyone as long as you say it in the right way. We need to communicate God's truth as sweetly and compassionately as possible.

In 2 Timothy 2:24–26 Paul says, "And the Lord's bond-servant must not be quarrelsome, but be kind to all, able to teach, patient when wronged, with gentleness correcting those who are in opposition, if perhaps God may grant them repentance leading to the knowledge of the truth, and they may come to their senses and escape from the snare of the devil, having been held captive by him to do his will" (NASB).

In my witnessing I must be gentle, kind, and gracious, but uncompromising as I share the Gospel message. I must let God do His work on His time schedule and at His prompting. When I told Linda the truth about the lifestyle she led, I didn't diminish anything. My message to her was strong, but I made sure it was lovingly and gently given.

——————— ✑ ———————

A second tool we can rely upon as we witness is a lifestyle that confirms and affirms we have a relationship to the Lord Jesus Christ. Lost men don't know we are His disciples by our doctrine! They don't understand doctrine because there is a veil over their eyes, but they can know we belong to Christ through the love we show toward one another. Does your life demonstrate His love? If you love Him, you'll love others and you'll keep His commandments. Remember Jesus came to save us from our sins. As Anthony Evans, a professor at Dallas Theological Seminary, says, "Sinners are supposed to sin; it's in their job description." It's not in ours! Righteousness is in our job description. If you are harboring sin in your life, you're going to lack confidence and power when it comes to sharing the Gospel.

BEARING FRUIT

Someone once told me that an apple tree bears apples not by striving to bear apples but simply by the very nature of what it is. The more deeply I abide in the Vine (Christ), the more fruit will abound in my life, and the more naturally I will share Him.

—Carole

As Joseph Aldrich teaches in *Life-Style Evangelism* (Multnomah), many need to hear the melody of the Gospel before they are ready to hear its word. Your life is the melody others hear. Believe me, others are watching how you think and react. I've had people tell me that they were watching me to see if I was real. At our summer teen "Boot Camp" I heard many teens tell how carefully they watched the Christian kids in their schools, churches, or even at "Boot Camp" to see if what they had was genuine, if it made a difference. When they saw it did, then they wanted Jesus also.

———— ✑ ————

Prayer is a third, and vital, tool at our disposal as we go about sharing the Gospel. The importance of prayer preceding and accompanying our witness is absolutely crucial. As I sat through the early morning hours with my friend in Europe, I was inwardly groaning in prayer, crying out, begging God to turn her from darkness and the power of Satan. And as I shared, my traveling companion Jean Galloway would intercede; then when Jean shared with her, I'd intercede.

Prayer also opens doors for us so that we can even have the opportunity to share. I once heard the story of a group of missionaries in South America who were presenting the Gospel yet getting nowhere. Not until they started praying, until they began to stand against the forces of Satan with prayer, did they begin to see incredible results.

———— ✑ ————

The fourth and final tool we can call upon as we witness is the skill of listening. Listening is essential. Engage people in conversation. Then let them talk. Listen to where they're coming from. As you listen, ask God to give you insight in how to meet them biblically where they are. After all, the Word of God has the answer for every situation of life. As they hear the practicality of the Word, God can use that to draw them to himself.

As you read through the Gospels, you'll find Jesus meeting people at their point of felt need, then taking them from there to the all-important matter of their relationship to Him. Watch how Jesus deals with Nicodemus in John 3 or the woman at the well in John 4. While He deals with each differently, He begins at their point of need, their point of interest.

Not long ago, I had a forty-minute ride in a taxi from the airport to my mother's home in a neighboring city. Besides the driver, one other passenger, a young man, joined me for the trip. As we rode along in the dark, I felt convicted that I needed to share Jesus Christ. But getting started does not come naturally for me, for, as I said, I don't have the gift of evangelism.

I prayed and then jumped in. I started to ask general questions of both the driver and the other passenger. Soon, we got around to talking about families, and I discovered that both of these men were in the midst of marriages that were breaking up. Both were really hurting. With that, I found my point of identification. Having gone through a divorce myself before I came to Christ, I could surmise some of what they were going through. I told them I knew what the pain felt like, that I had once been in their shoes. I then slipped into the Gospel. I didn't get as far as I would have liked, but I did get their addresses and was able to mail them some follow-up material.

On that day, I was there to plant a seed. Sometimes, all we can do is plow the ground and get it ready for the seed. Usually I plow and sow. Very rarely do I see people come to Christ one-on-one. When I teach, I see many come to the Lord, but that's different from witnessing. That's harvest time. Whatever—plowing, sowing, or watering, I need to remember it is "God who causes the growth" (1 Corinthians 3:7, NASB).

———— ✐ ————

One reason we fear witnessing is because we assume we must witness to every person who crosses our path. If we don't, we feel like failures. Relax. Let the Holy Spirit lead you. The approach that has worked best for me is to go about witnessing with the mindset of "Lord, if you want me to share with this person, show me how to open the door."

Our goal in sharing the Gospel need not always be a decision. A witness is someone who testifies. I am not called to save anyone. Sometimes we are to start a work that will be finished much later. Salvation is of the Lord. If I can remember that I'm simply to testify to the Gospel of Jesus Christ whenever and however I get the chance, and that the power to do so comes from the Holy Spirit who resides within me, then I can indeed go out and confidently spread the Good News.

Make It Happen

1. While written handouts can be a help as you witness, be cautious that they don't become a crutch. Find out why the person you are witnessing to is saying "yes." If a person only wants out of his misery but hasn't confronted his sin, he may be no more ready to accept

Christ than he was before you shared with him. Relax, and let God work on His timetable.

2. Remember, the burden of salvation is not yours. You don't save people, God does. And likewise, you don't lose people if they don't say "yes" to your efforts. Share as the Lord leads you and don't be overly concerned about the "bottom line."

3. Prepare yourself for witnessing by studying your Bible. If it helps, select several verses you would use to lead a person through the Gospel. Write them out, and, if possible, commit them to memory—if not the words, then their location. Some verses to consider include: John 3:16–18, Romans 3:23 or 6:23, and 1 Timothy 1:15.

4. Pray for confidence in sharing the Gospel and for doors to open. Realize witnessing can be a formidable challenge, but look at all the wonderful tools and support that the Lord gives us. Keep your focus on those and how vital it is for others to know of the saving grace of our Lord.

Do You Speak a Foreign Language?

Judith Couchman

You don't need to master a spiritual vocabulary to share your faith. In fact, you'll probably communicate better without it. Many nonbelievers don't have a Christian background. Or if they do, religious words may conjure up unwanted memories.

To keep from scaring somebody away, check your Christian jargon and eliminate what's not necessary. Spiritual words can be divided into the following categories:

Unchangeable. Certain words reflect the Gospel's heartbeat: sin, salvation, love, grace. You'd be remiss to lead someone to Christ without using them. Fortunately, nonbelievers also are familiar with these words; they express *love*, are *saved* from harm, use *grace* periods on insurance bills. So use them, explaining them as necessary.

Translatable. Phrases such as "washed in the blood," "fellowship of believers," or "equipping the saints," are biblical. But your unbelieving friend might misunderstand them. You can easily express these important concepts with other words.

Cultural. Somewhere in church history believers adopted these and tenaciously wrung them until all meaning drained out. Why do we "lift up in prayer to the throne of grace" or "share what's on our hearts"? I doubt if anyone knows. Certainly not your unsaved friend!

While nothing's a guarantee, these guidelines also might help you communicate clearly:

Ask about the person's religious background. It's a way to measure her understanding of Christian vocabulary.

Substitute words as often as possible. If you flourish with words like "propitiation" and "trespasses," a listener may be turned off. If you try "a substitute" and "wrongdoings," you may keep someone's attention longer.

Explain yourself. If the person looks puzzled, ask, "Did I say something you don't understand?" Casually define a term when you say it. Discover what certain words mean to your friend.

Increase biblical language in proportion to spiritual hunger. As your friend grows more interested in Christianity, she'll be less offended by its vocabulary. Introduce scriptural terms when they're palatable.

Keep a sense of humor. Remember, you're speaking a foreign language to a nonbeliever. There's bound to be occasional mess-ups—but with a little sensitivity and common sense, your message should be clear.

—From *Today's Christian Woman* (March/April 1990)

EPILOGUE

NEVER-ENDING JOURNEY

OUR INDIVIDUAL SPIRITUAL JOURNEYS will be as unique as our fingerprints. In our quest for spiritual maturity, some of us will take frequent side trips, others will shoot forward in a direct line from point A to point B, and still others will move along in stops and starts. Yet, however we reach our destination, there are three rules of the road we all must heed.

First and foremost, we must seek to have a relationship with our Savior. The primary elements for this relationship to flourish are time together on a daily basis and continual, two-way communication through prayer and worship. When we ignore these basics we can be certain we'll never reach our destination. May the many stories and insights of Kay, Jill, and Carole serve to inspire you and convince you not to delay one more moment in putting these basics in place in your life.

Second, we should never underestimate the force of the enemy as we seek to nurture our relationship with God. We need to navigate defensively throughout our spiritual journey, for if we let our defenses down we leave opportunities for Satan to push us off the road. As soon as you feel yourself pulled to the right or left of the road, take action for, as Kay said, "We are at warfare."

And finally, if we hope to have a fulfilling spiritual life, we must know the Word of God. Kay, Carole, and Jill repeat this vital theme throughout the pages of this book and, while it might seem simple, it is a crucial truth—for how else can we get to know God except through His Word. To know the Word of God means we must read it, study it, and take it to heart so that it literally becomes part of our being.

At whatever point you are in your spiritual journey, we hope this book has helped you find the answers you need to grow stronger in your faith, to deepen your relationship with the Lord, and, most of all, to inspire you to continue to grow into the woman God wants you to be.

———— ✍ ————

Today's Christian Woman is a positive, practical magazine designed for contemporary Christian women of all ages, single or married, who seek to live out biblical values in their homes, workplaces, and communities. With honesty and warmth, *Today's Christian Woman* provides depth, balance, and perspective to the issues that confront women today.

If you would like a subscription to *Today's Christian Woman* send your name and address to:

TODAY'S CHRISTIAN WOMAN
P.O. Box 11618
Des Moines, IA 50340

Subscription rates:
one year (6 issues) $14.95
two years (12 issues) $23.60